Taoist Nei Dan
Inner Meditation

by the same author

The Luo Collaterals
A Handbook for Clinical Practice and Treating Emotions
and the Shen and The Six Healing Sounds
ISBN 978 1 84819 230 0
eISBN 978 0 85701 219 7

The Divergent Channels – Jing Bie
A Handbook for Clinical Practice and Five Shen Nei Dan Inner Meditation
ISBN 978 1 84819 189 1
eISBN 978 0 85701 150 3

Eight Extraordinary Channels – Qi Jing Ba Mai
A Handbook for Clinical Practice and Nei Dan Inner Meditation
ISBN 978 1 84819 148 8
eISBN 978 0 85701 137 4

I Ching Acupuncture – The Balance Method
Clinical Applications of the Ba Gua and I Ching
ISBN 978 1 84819 074 0
eISBN 978 0 85701 064 3

TAOIST NEI DAN
INNER MEDITATION

An Accessible Guide

Dr David Twicken, DOM, L.Ac.

SINGING DRAGON
LONDON AND PHILADELPHIA

First published in Great Britain in 2023 by Singing Dragon,
an imprint of Jessica Kingsley Publishers
Part of John Murray Press

2

Copyright © David Twicken 2023

Front cover image source: Deposit Photos.

A CIP catalogue record for this title is available from the
British Library and the Library of Congress

ISBN 978 1 83997 387 1
eISBN 978 1 83997 388 8

Printed and bound in the United States by Integrated Books International

Jessica Kingsley Publishers' policy is to use papers that are natural,
renewable and recyclable products and made from wood grown in
sustainable forests. The logging and manufacturing processes are expected
to conform to the environmental regulations of the country of origin.

Singing Dragon
Carmelite House
50 Victoria Embankment
London EC4Y 0DZ

www.singingdragon.com

John Murray Press
Part of Hodder & Stoughton Limited
An Hachette UK Company

Contents

Disclaimer

The information in this book is based on the author's knowledge and personal experience. It is presented for educational purposes to assist the reader in expanding his or her knowledge of Chinese philosophy and medicine. The techniques and practices are to be used at the reader's own discretion and liability. The author is not responsible in any manner whatsoever for any physical injury that may occur as a result of following instructions in this book. Please consult a licensed medical practitioner before beginning any of the practices in this book.

Acknowledgments

I have been fortunate to study with some very special people. One common quality among all of them was their encouragement to study a wide range of teachings. A special thank you goes to Master Mantak Chia for sharing Qi gong, meditation, nei dan internal alchemy and Taoism with compassion, respect and love to anybody with a desire to learn. You are a treasure.

I would like to give special thanks to Master Mary Chow, who taught me how to bring joy and love to practicing Tai Chi Chuan; to Master Joseph Yu for sharing the importance of studying classics and learning to apply them in practice; and]

A big thank you and hug to my friend and colleague Fritz Hudnit, DAOM, L.Ac., for your editing contribution.

A big thank you to my friends and colleagues Ariana Accardi, L.Ac., and Janel Gehrke, DAOM, L.Ac., for your editorial contributions.

Dynasty Years

Pre-historic period	
Yangshao	5000 BC
Longshan	2500 BC
Xia	2100–1600 BC
Historic period	
Shang	1600–1045 BC
Zhou	1045–221 BC
Western Zhou	1045–771 BC
Eastern Zhou	770–256 BC
Spring and Autumn Period	722–481 BC
Warring States Period	403–221 BC
Qin	221–206 BC
Han	206 BC–AD 220
Western Han	206 BC–AD 24
Eastern Han	AD 25–220
Three Kingdoms	220–280

cont.

Historic period	
Jin (Western and Eastern)	265–420
Southern and Northern	420–589
Sui	581–618
Tang	618–907
Five Dynasties and Ten Kingdoms	907–960
Song	960–1279
Liao	916–1125
Jin	1115–1234
Yuan	1271–1368
Ming	1368–1644
Qing (Manchu)	1644–1911
Republic of China	1912–1949
People's Republic of China	1949–present

From the Author

Taoist nei dan is a gift from enlightened ancient people that has been passed down from generation to generation. It is a series of movements, breath work and meditations that focus on benefiting three main aspects of life: physical health, psycho-emotional balance and spiritual realization. Nei dan is a self-cultivation practice that is designed to enhance daily life. Changes in daily life are a sign that nei dan is working. Nei dan is a path to attune to your true nature. And within attuning is realignment and a crystallization of body, mind and spirit. A fruit of nei dan is being a living expression of spirit; it is living from spirit. Living from spirit is also called living in the Tao, living in the light, Christ consciousness and Buddha mind. Living from spirit is the most natural way of living. I hope this book assists you in living a natural life.

Introduction

Meditation is practiced around the world to seek peace, balance, emotional harmony, vitality and spiritual connection. There are many styles and methods of meditation. In ancient China, a system of meditation (nei dan) developed that influences the three treasures: body, mind and spirit. Some nei dan inner meditation approaches focus more on one treasure than another or on some combination of the three. Nei dan literally means inner pill; a pill in this context is medicine. Much like the ingredients of a pill that cause a reaction within the body, nei dan is generally a series of meditations that cause a reaction in the three treasures. Nei dan can include postures—standing, sitting and lying—which are the external expressions. These external forms can be practiced in combination with inner meditation, as they assist the internal meditation by aligning the physical body to enhance the internal movements that occur in the nei dan inner meditation. A good nei dan system integrates both external and internal aspects of the practice to optimize results.

Taoist nei dan originated in ancient China. Nei dan is

integrated with the acupuncture channel system. That integration is what makes this form of nei dan unique and a primary reason it has significant health benefits. Nei dan can be a profound form of medical Qi gong. Qi means energy, life force and the body's bioelectricity; those three terms are used interchangeably in this book. There is no clear and definitive translation of Qi that is understandable in English, but knowing what it does provides a practical understanding. Gong means art, skill, work, cultivation, mastery. Qi gong is the skill, art and mastery of life force, the energy in our body and all around us. Nei dan is a powerful method of cultivation—the working with and mastering of the life force primarily inside our body for health, vitality and spiritual realization.

A Diamond in the Rough

A diamond in the rough is an image that illustrates how the process of Shen realization (self-realization) can occur. Each person has a diamond. The diamond is their Shen (spirit). The rough includes the stresses, conditioning, imprints, patterns, emotions and unfavorable influences that occur in life. We all have a diamond shining within, and we all have the "rough." The amount and types of the rough vary among people. Nei dan inner meditation can assist in releasing, clearing and removing the rough, thereby allowing insight and alignment with the diamond. This process can be life-changing and can provide additional inspiration and motivation for further changes. It can inspire a person to live in a way that allows synchronization with Shen (by becoming aware of it) and becoming a living expression of Shen.

Jing–Shen

The Chinese understood that life experiences could shift awareness away from Shen. Sometimes there are minor shifts, and sometimes there are major shifts. These people expressed their understanding of the integration of the relationship of Shen and individual life experiences with the term *Jing–Shen*. Jing from this perspective is the physical body and the experiences we have processed and retained in our body–mind. It is these experiences and our response to them that can either maintain our Shen awareness or cause a shift away from it. Jing–Shen contains the accumulation of experiences and their influences on our life. In spiritual cultivation, a goal is to clear away or understand the experiences in our life that cause a Shen disturbance. This process can allow Shen realization. Each person's unique life experiences and their responses to them determine the degree of nei dan practice necessary to release from attachments to the rough and align to their spirit.

Jing–Shen is one inseparable whole; each influences the other. Our experiences of life are stored in Jing, and Jing influences our capacity to experience Shen. Jing influences how we perceive, respond to and interact with all aspects of our life. This symbiotic relationship reflects the way we experience life based on the environment while in the womb, our early childhood experiences and conditioning from our family and society. The body processes these experiences, and if all is well, they are filtered in a way that allows us to grow, mature and develop in a favorable way. Sometimes our experiences are difficult and can be traumatic. Jing holds the experiences (often they are held when they should be let go), which can then influence our ability to connect and align with the present moment and Shen. When we live from these past experiences, we are trapped in the past. Living in the past prevents us from living in the spontaneity of life. As nei dan practitioners, we can apply the methods of balance found in Taoist philosophy and Chinese medicine to assist a person in restoring balance and harmony in their life by reducing/releasing the held, unfavorable experiences. This releasing can allow awareness and natural expression of Shen, which is a key aspect of nei dan inner meditation.

The nei dan practices presented in this book are easy to learn and practice. They can assist in releasing stagnation, trauma and conditioning (the rough) that may have entered deep inside a person (Jing–Shen); they can also attune a person to their diamond (spirit). This attuning or spiritual realization is often called special, unique, spiritual or mystical; in reality, it is our normal, natural state of being. The nei dan practices in this book offer practical approaches to assist a person in achieving physical health, psycho-emotional balance and spiritual realization.

CHAPTER 1

The Shen

Lao Zi is considered the founder of philosophical Taoism. The *Tao Teh Ching* by Lao Zi is one of the most translated books in the world. The book describes the Way (Tao). It includes a profound description of what occurs when we do not follow the Way. The descriptions include a range of reactions to daily life, including emotional responses and psychological conditions. If the root of these responses and conditions is not changed, they can lead to a Shen disturbance. Lao Zi offers advice on how to find balance and live a natural life, which is the path to living in harmony with the Way. Chinese medicine identifies exogenous and endogenous factors that influence the body, mind and spirit, causing a Shen disturbance. The insights and life guidance from Lao Zi and Chinese medicine presented in this book can assist in treating Shen disturbances. Integrating the two provides an effective framework for understanding and working with emotional imbalances and Shen disturbances.

The Way

The ancient Chinese people studied nature deeply. They perceived the cycles of human development and nature's endless flows and cycles. They observed the visible world. They were also able to perceive the invisible forces happening within the visible world, and they mapped out the invisible energetic forces of nature. They understood that the invisible and the visible are one inseparable whole. These ancient people viewed the creator and creation as one. The creative force of the universe is within all of life. The Chinese named the entire process, function and structure of the world the *Tao*. The Tao includes the invisible forces and visible forms of the world. The cycles and flows of the visible world contain an energetic force, which they called *Qi*, which is part of the Tao. All of life is the Tao, and the Tao is within all of life. When a person is aware of this reality, they are aware of the Tao within themselves. The Tao within each person includes the Shen. A definition of a *Shen separation or disturbance* includes no awareness of the Tao (Shen). This lack of awareness can arise from a deep polarity within a person and is a main cause of illness. Humans have the capability of attaching their focus to their thoughts, opinions, beliefs and emotions; the nature and degree of those attachments are the cause of internal polarity and separation from their spirit.

The *Tao Teh Ching* is the foundation for all traditions of Tao. The following is from Chapter 25 of the *Tao Teh Ching*:

Before Heaven and Earth are born,
there is something formless and complete in itself.

Impalpable and everlasting, silent and undisturbed,

standing alone and unchanging.

It exercises itself gently,

and generates itself inexhaustibly in all dimensions.

It may be regarded as the Mother of all things.

Far beyond humans' relative conception,

it cannot be referred to by a specific name.

Yet it may be identified as the Tao,

the subtle truth of the universe.

Expressing its integral nature,

Tao remains intangible, yielding, and uncontrollable: the ultimate
    expression of the cosmos.

As an expression of its unceasing creativeness,

it first manifests as the spaciousness of the sky.

As an expression of its receptiveness,

it manifests second as the great massiveness of galaxies, stars, and
    planets.

As a further expression of its harmonious reintegration,

it manifests third as human life.

Thus, in the natural flow of energy transformation,

human life becomes one of the four great expressions of the path of
    subtle universal integration.

Humankind conforms itself to Earth.

Earth conforms itself to the sky.

The sky conforms itself to the Subtle Origin.

The Subtle Origin conforms to its own nature.[1]

---

1   Ni, H.-C. (1979) *The Complete Works of Lao Tzu*. Chapter 25. Malibu, CA: The Shrine of the Eternal Breath of Tao.

This chapter of the *Tao Teh Ching* includes the insight that the creator of the universe is also within its creation. When someone conforms and aligns oneself with earth (the Tao), they realize that they are part of creation and inseparable from the Tao. The process of conforming, aligning and attuning to Shen is called "Shen realization." The ancient Chinese have developed numerous ways to assist in Shen realization. The ways include meditation, nei dan (inner alchemy), prayer, Qi gong, dance, acupuncture, herbal medicine and reading classics (*I Ching*, *Tao Teh Ching*, etc.). Some of the Shen realization methods are simple, and some of them are very complex. A variety of ways to assist a person in Shen realization is presented in the following chapters.

The Shen in the *Nei Jing Ling Shu* Medical Text

"Shen" can be translated as "spirit." The ancient Chinese often described Shen in non-direct ways. Instead of focusing on specific descriptions of Shen, they focused on how to experience Shen. Their focus is on Shen realization. They developed methods for people to practice (cultivation) that could guide them to Shen realization. In Chapter 54 of the *Nei Jing Ling Shu*, "The Allotted Year of a Human's Life," Qi Bo is asked about the meaning of spirit (Shen). Qi Bo states:

When one's blood and energy are complete and harmonized, when nourishing and protective Qi are complete and penetrating, when the five viscera are complete and matured, the spirit

Qi is sheltered in the Heart and mind, and the animal spirit and human soul complete the organs, the person is complete.[2]

My interpretation of Qi Bo's answer is the following. Blood, nourishing Qi and the animal spirit are Yin. Qi, wei Qi and the human soul are Yang. The Heart and mind are Yang, and the organs are Yin. When Yin and Yang are in harmony, vital substances, organs and emotions are in harmony, and the body and spirit are unified. This unification can lead to the following insight: when we are in balance and in harmony within ourselves and the world around us, our body and spirit naturally unify and we become a living expression of spirit, and we are then complete. Shen realization is awareness of our most primary nature. This awareness is often called "aliveness." Taoists understand this aliveness as the most natural and fundamental aspect of a person. Qi gong, nei dan, acupuncture, herbal medicine and the *Tao Teh Ching* and the *I Ching* are ways to assist a person in their Shen realization.

Aliveness is described in a variety of ways. The most meaningful description is *present awareness*. When we are aware, we are present with our aliveness. Thoughts, feelings and opinions appear and disappear; present awareness always exists. Present awareness is the Tao, and it is the Shen. Being fully aware (mindful of present awareness) is Shen realization.

Qi Bo describes what makes a person complete. *When we realize we are present awareness, we are complete. When we attach*

---

2 Wu, J. (2002) *Ling Shu or The Spiritual Pivot*. Chapter 54. Honolulu, HI: University of Hawai'i Press.

our identity to anything that is not present awareness, we are incomplete. The severity of the attachment is a major cause of Shen disturbance.

In the long history of China, there have been numerous explanations of the cause of illness and Shen disturbances. The main causes according to early Chinese culture are presented below.

Early Chinese Culture and Illness

The Shang dynasty is the first historic period of China. As in most ancient cultures, there was a belief in supernatural intervention. This belief is the basis of theurgic medicine. An example of theurgic medicine in China is the "curse of the ancestors," which is the first main explanation of illness in the Shang dynasty. This explanation includes the belief that there is a relationship between the living and the dead, and that if a living person attacked or harmed another living person, the harmed person's ancestors would harm the attacker, causing illness. We could evaluate this theory as a cultural explanation to guide people's behavior. The goal is to get people to act in ways that create harmony among the living. With harmony on earth, there would be harmony with the ancestors.

In the Zhou dynasty, the second historic period, a new explanation of illness was introduced. During the Warring States period (403–221 BC) of the Zhou dynasty, civil war occurred in China. This period was the most violent in its history. The Chin tribe and its leader Ying Zheng were at the center of the

Warring States period. Ying Zheng's goal was to conquer all the tribes in the country and unify China under his sole control. Within this unification, he would become the first emperor of China. The Warring States period included violent chaos. In the Chinese view, the violent chaos on earth caused violent chaos in the heavens (the ancestors). The chaos broke the direct bond between the living and the ancestors. This broken bond led to demons or ghosts, which did not follow any ancestor relationship. The ghosts or demons could attack anybody in the same way that the warring armies attacked anybody in their pursuit of defeating all on their way to total domination. Curse of the ancestors and attack of demons became a main explanation of illness and Shen disturbance at that time, and exorcism became a main treatment method; both are found in the oldest known Chinese medical book—the Mawangdui medical texts. These medical texts are from the Warring States period of the Zhou dynasty.

From the Warring States period to the Han dynasty, there was a transformation in Chinese medicine. The Han dynasty classics, the *Nei Jing Su Wen* and the *Nei Jing Ling Shu*, developed from the Mawangdui medical texts. Practitioners later added new and more detailed information about nature, the human body and the acupuncture channels. Most importantly, practitioners added acupuncture points that comprise a key part of the *Su Wen* and the *Ling Shu*. One area in which the *Su Wen* and the *Ling Shu* shifted away from the Mawangdui texts was the belief in curse of the ancestors and demons as a cause of illness. The *Su Wen* and the *Ling Shu* medical texts include a

sophisticated analysis of the causes of illness based on genetics (Jing), external pathogenic factors, internal pathogens and
lifestyle. There is a magnificent presentation of the cycles and
patterns of nature in the classics (see Chapters 66–71 of the *Su
Wen*). The *Su Wen* presents cycles of days, months and years
that create pathogens not commonly known to the average
person or medical practitioner; these are called atmospheric
influences. It is possible to view genetic/Jing conditions as a
type of curse of the ancestors. If demons are viewed as illnesses
or conditions that arise from an unknown cause, the pathogens
created by the invisible (atmospheric influences) in the cycles
of time can be viewed as a variation of the influence of demons
or ghosts. These cycles of nature are a more modern way of
explaining these unknown influences.

In early Chinese philosophy books, as well as the classic medical texts, the *Su Wen* and the *Ling Shu*, Shen is often explained
in nebulous ways. The books generally explain the actions
of life that cause an imbalance of Shen, and ways to restore
balance and harmony. In the *Su Wen* and the *Ling Shu*, there
are detailed diagnoses based on Chinese medical principles.
When a person has a Shen disturbance, the condition is usually
explained using Chinese medical patterns and syndromes—for
example, Liver fire or phlegm misting the Heart. A treatment
is then made based on Chinese medical principles. Treatment
can include herbs, acupuncture, dao yin (Qi gong), nutrition
and lifestyle guidance. The contributors to the *Nei Jing* do not
deny that there are other causes of Shen disturbance, but they
present a significant and profound model of evaluation that

allows the practitioner to apply healing methods within the *Nei Jing* medical system that may help a certain percentage of people. For other causes of Shen imbalances, therapy, spiritual guidance and Western medicine can be an important part of the treatment and healing process.

Chinese and Taoist healers have several ways of viewing Shen. A common way is viewing the overall condition of a person: for example, their Shen is strong and balanced, or the Shen is disturbed and imbalanced. The Shen can also be viewed in two aspects—Yin–Yang and the Hun and Po. The Hun is the Yang and ethereal aspect of a person, and the Po is the Yin and corporeal aspect. Another way to view Shen is the *five shen*. The five shen is an important medical framework for diagnosis and treatment; it is also an integral aspect of nei dan. The five shen will be presented in detail in this book. The healing sounds and the five shen nei dan inner meditation are the nei dan practices that focus on the five shen cultivation.

Aliveness

All of humanity shares the experience of living on planet Earth; it can be called *aliveness*. Every person can have *awareness* of this aliveness. This awareness is often described as mystical, magical and transcendental. In reality, it is the most natural and normal part of life. This aliveness is Shen. It is also called the Original Shen (Original Spirit). Chinese spiritual, medical and nei dan traditions have numerous ways to assist a person in attuning to this aliveness. Stress, trauma and conditioning (life experiences) that occur in our life can shift our consciousness away from awareness of aliveness. Nei dan practices assist in attuning to our aliveness (spirit). Nei dan guides a person to experience the most fundamental aspect of themselves—not something unique, special and distant—which is a reason for its effectiveness.

CHAPTER 2

The Five Shen

Chinese culture is one of the most diverse in the world. Chinese traditions include indigenous culture, shamanism, Taoism, Confucianism, Buddhism and combinations of all of them. Each tradition has a unique insight about life. And each tradition has an understanding of spirit. The Chinese word for spirit is "Shen." From a macro viewpoint, each person has one Shen. We can view the totality of a person in terms of one Shen. For example, we might say that person has a vibrant Shen. We might also say they have a Shen disharmony. The term Shen encompasses the collective psycho-emotional condition of a person. The Chinese also view the Shen as multi-dimensional. The multi-dimensional view of a person is described by the *five shen*.

Chinese medicine offers a model that can view each person both as a whole and in its component parts, which allows insight about these two aspects of a person. A person can be viewed in terms of their physical parts to target their physical condition. For example, a medical practitioner can evaluate a person's muscles, bones, arteries, veins, glands and internal organs to identify which of these may be diseased. The Shen can also be evaluated according to its parts. Viewing the Shen both as the collective condition of a person and in its parts (its multi-dimensional sub-forms) is part of Chinese spiritual and medical traditions. The contributors to the *Ling Shu* and the *Su Wen* left a road map of these traditions; both are valuable in clinical practice and nei dan.

Tai Chi is a model to explain how the universe (Tao) functions. Tai Chi contains three forces: Yang, Yuan and Yin. In Figure 2.1 the white color is Yang, the black color is Yin and the curved line down the middle is Yuan. Yuan is the original force; in this case, it is the original energy. This original energy can be understood in terms of expansion into Yin and Yang, and yet the three forces are really one integrated force. These three forces interact to create an infinite number of patterns that comprise the universe.

FIGURE 2.1 THE TAI CHI SYMBOL

This is the macrocosmic view of Tai Chi. A microcosmic view is that the Tao divides the whole into three component parts known as the *three treasures*. These treasures are Jing, Qi and Shen. Like the three forces in the Tai Chi symbol, the three treasures are inseparable; however, each treasure can be viewed, evaluated and treated as an individual treasure. Each treasure can also be viewed as one part of an interrelated process where each one influences the others.

The human body contains a variety of Yin–Yang pairs, including acupuncture channels and organs, the front and back of the body, and the arms and legs. Likewise, the Shen can be understood in terms of its *relationship* to the organs. The relationship of the Shen to the organs is represented as the five shen. Chinese medicine includes a unique insight that the organs house the five shen (explained below). This insight is an example of the interrelationship between the body and mind (spirit).

Chinese medicine distinguishes the functions and imbalances of the Shen from the five shen. A way to communicate this difference is to capitalize the S in "Shen" when referring to the collective aspect of the spirit. The five shen will be lower case: for example, the shen, the yi, the po, the zhi and the hun of the Heart, Spleen, Lungs, Kidneys and the Liver. The five shen are five aspects of the one Shen. Each of the five organs also has a function and role in health and vitality. Most interestingly, the ancient healers perceived the resonance between the organs and the psycho-emotional condition. These healers created the five shen Chinese medical model to explain this relationship. It is one of the earliest understandings of the mind–body relationship.

The following passage from Chapter 5 of the *Su Wen* describes a relationship between nature, the internal organs and the five shen:

> Nature contains the four seasons and the five phases of wood, fire, earth, metal, and water. The five phases interact, change, and transform to create cold, summer heat, damp, dryness, and wind. The weather affects everything in the natural world and is the foundation for the cycle of life: birth, growth, maturation, and death. In the human body there are the five yin (zang) internal organs of the Heart, Spleen, Lungs, Kidneys, and the Liver. The organs provide the structure and the Qi to form and allow the manifestation of the five spirits, which then gives rise to the five natural virtues and emotions.[1]

This *Su Wen* passage explains the materialization of the five shen in the body. The description expresses the relationship between the cosmos and humanity: the macrocosm and microcosm. Chapter 8 of the *Ling Shu* presents the five shen and their relationships to the five Yin organs. The psychological, emotional and mental qualities of each organ are presented. The condition of the organs can influence the five shen and their related areas of life; conversely, the condition of the five shen (psycho-emotional) can influence the organs. For example,

---

1   Ni, M. (1995) *The Yellow Emperor's Classic of Medicine: A New Translation of NeiJing Suwen with Commentary.* Chapter 5. Boston, MA: Shambhala.

fear can manifest if someone has a chronic Kidney deficiency. That *Ling Shu* reference describes the interrelationship between the Yin organs and the five shen. The Yin organs create the structure for the five shen to manifest in life, which includes their corresponding virtues. The organs provide the physical structure for the five shen to exist in the body. This is a foundation relationship for the body–mind–spirit relationship and holistic medicine.

The five shen medical model provides a clinically effective framework to treat psycho-emotional conditions. It provides a system that enables the practitioner to match specific psycho-emotional conditions to their corresponding channels, points, vital substances and energy centers in the body. These relationships allow the practitioner to customize a treatment for each patient. They also allow a nei dan practitioner to focus on specific practices for particular stagnations, blockages and the rough.

I have found there are two main ways to diagnose a Shen condition. The first is by assessing the overall condition of a person, and the second is by assessing the five shen. One or more of the five shen can be imbalanced. A goal in treatment is to restore each of the five shen, creating a balanced Shen.

The five shen model enables the healing or nei dan practitioner to make a targeted treatment (practice), which in my experience is more effective than applying only a general Shen treatment/practice. In the practice of acupuncture, treating any of the five shen with their corresponding luo point is a direct way to influence that organ/shen correspondence, and the nei dan practitioner can practice the healing sounds in the same way. This method is effective when the psycho-emotional condition is active and disturbing. It is also an effective way to assist in releasing repressed emotions and experiences, especially when combined with other nei dan practices (this is explained throughout the book).

The *Ling Shu* and the *Su Wen* include detailed information about the five shen. The following section explains the foundation for a "five shen" diagnosis and treatment plan. A treatment plan can include acupuncture and nei dan practices.

The Five Shen

Chapter 5 of the *Su Wen*, "The Manifestation of Yin and Yang from the Macrocosm to the Microcosm," presents the five shen. The five shen are a model for understanding patterns of disharmony. The ancients understood that the Yin organs house the five shen; Yang (shen) must have Yin (organs) to contain it. The conditions of the five shen can influence the Yin organs, and the conditions of the Yin organs can influence the five shen.

A strategy for diagnosis is matching emotions to their corresponding shen and organ. In the metaphor of the diamond in the rough, imbalances of these emotions are the rough. Nei dan practices can clear the roughness, revealing the shining light of the diamond (i.e. the Shen). Awareness of your Shen can inspire, motivate and provide the incentive for change and transformation. Once you know what you are (Shen), you then know what you are not. This realization plays an essential role in realigning to one's true nature when life's stresses pull one away from living in present awareness.

Five Shen Resonances

Five shen resonances (correspondences) tell us much about the nature of the five shen. The main resonances are from the *Ling Shu*, Chapter 8, "Roots and Spirit," and the *Su Wen*, Chapter 5, "The Manifestation of Yin and Yang from the Macrocosm to the Microcosm."

The Twelve Organs

The Heart is the sovereign of all organs and represents the consciousness of one's spirit. It is responsible for intelligence, wisdom and spiritual transformation.

The Lung is the advisor. It helps the Heart in regulating the Qi.

The Liver is like the general. It is intelligent and courageous.

The Gallbladder is like a judge. It has the power of discrimination.

The Pericardium is like the court jester. He makes the emperor laugh, bringing joy.

The Stomach and Spleen are like warehouses; they store food and essences. They digest, transform and transport food and nutrients.

The Large Intestine transports turbidity (waste products).

The Small Intestine receives the food that has been digested by the Spleen and Stomach; it further extracts, absorbs and transports the food's essences from the extraction process throughout the body. It separates the pure from the turbid.

The Kidneys store vitality. This mobilizes the four extremities. The Kidneys also benefit the memory, willpower and coordination.

The San Jiao promotes the transformation and transportation of fluids throughout the body.

The Bladder is where water converges and is eliminated.

The Five Storehouses

The Liver is the storehouse of blood, and it is the shelter of the human soul (hun spirit).

The Spleen is the storehouse of nourishment, and it is the shelter of thought (yi spirit).

The Heart is the storehouse for the channels, and it is the shelter of the spirit (shen spirit).

The Lung is the storehouse of Qi, and it is the shelter of the animal spirit (po spirit).

The Kidneys are the storehouse of the seminal essence, and they are the shelter of the will (zhi spirit).

The Five Shen and Their Inherent Qualities

The spirit of the Heart is called the shen, and it rules mental and creative functions.

The spirit of the Liver is called the hun, and it rules the nervous system and gives rise to extrasensory awareness.

The spirit of the Spleen is known as the yi, and it rules logic and rational thought.

The spirit of the Lungs is called the po, and it rules the animalistic instincts, as well as physical strength and endurance.

The spirit of the Kidneys is called the zhi, and it rules the will, drive, ambition and the survival instinct.

The Five Shen and Emotions

Anger can injure the Liver, but sadness can relieve anger. Metal controls wood. The po controls the hun.

Too much joy can cause a depletion of the Heart Qi; this can be counterbalanced by fear. Water controls fire. The zhi controls the shen.

Excessive worry will deplete Spleen Qi, but anger can restrain this worry. Wood controls earth. The hun controls the yi.

Extreme grief can injure the Lungs; but it may be countered by the emotion of happiness. Fire controls metal. The shen controls the po.

Fear and fright will damage the Kidneys. They can be defeated with understanding, logic and rational thinking. Earth controls water. The yi controls the zhi.

In applying the last set of five-phases relationships, the controlling cycle is identified to treat an imbalance. In my experience, when the controlling cycle is in balance, the controlling phase shapes the controlled phase. For example, the zhi (water) shapes the shen (fire). It shapes it by sending its balanced energy and virtues to the Heart (shen), bringing it into balance. This shaping occurs for all the five shen. That approach is especially applied in the inner-smile and five shen nei dan meditations.

Some practitioners apply this controlling (shaping) theory to the five acupuncture transporting points to treat emotional conditions. The Han dynasty classic medical text, the *Nan Ching* (*The Classic of Difficulties*), introduces the five-phases points (the five element points); they are not presented in the *Su Wen* or the *Ling Shu*. In this method, the imbalanced organ is identified, and its controlling phase is needled. For example, if a person has anger and is irritable, Liver 4, Middle Seal, the metal point on the Liver channel, is treated to relieve anger. Anger can injure the Liver, but sadness can relieve anger. Sadness is the emotion of the Lungs, which is metal. Metal can relieve anger in this theory. This principle can be applied to all the channels. My preference is to use the child element if possible. In this case, fire is the child of wood, so the fire point is treated to reduce the anger of the Liver wood. It is a gentler way to reduce an excess condition.

The knowledge of each of the five shen has important clinical value. When there is an imbalance of the emotions, the practitioner can match the emotion to its corresponding organ and shen. These connections are the foundation for an organ and a five shen diagnosis and treatment plan.

The following insight from the *Ling Shu*, Chapter 8, "Roots and Spirit," is important in clinical practice and nei dan cultivation:

When the Heart and mind is frightened and full of distressed thoughts and anxiety, it can result in injury to the spirit. This can result in fear and loss of self.[2]

This quote can be interpreted in the following way: with stress and emotional turmoil, we can lose awareness and connection to self (spirit). Nei dan can assist in clearing or releasing the emotional attachment to the stress and turmoil. The release can assist in helping a person reconnect with their spirit. This process is self-realization.

The five shen are an example of the ancient healers' and spiritual practitioners' awareness of the unity of the body, mind and spirit. The key is to identify imbalances and the conditions that cause them. Often the emotional, psychological and spiritual condition reveals areas of life that a person needs to understand in order to grow. It is common for a person to act in a way that causes the imbalances to be expressed in their life; this expression may be necessary to raise awareness of the condition. The awareness provides an opportunity to recognize the situation and begin a path of change and transformation. The practice of Chinese medicine, including acupuncture, herbs, Qi gong and nei dan, can assist in this path of change, transformation and self-realization.

2   Wu, J. (2002) *Ling Shu or The Spiritual Pivot*. Chapter 8. Honolulu, HI: University of Hawai'i Press.

The Five Shen and Their Paired Organs

The five shen model includes the five Yin–Yang paired organs. For example, when the Heart shen is mentioned, it refers to the Heart and the Small Intestine. Below we look at each.

The Heart (Shen)

The Heart houses the Heart shen and the Shen; it is the fire system. The Heart shen corresponds to the physical and psycho-emotional conditions of the Heart organ. (The Shen is also called the Original Shen—the yuan shen, i.e. "the diamond.") Methods that connect a person to their Heart shen can provide the opportunity to realize knowledge, inspiration, wisdom and guidance regarding their spirit. Attuning to the Heart shen can bring direct experience of spirit and the inseparable nature of the universe. This unity exists for all people. In Chinese culture, living from this awareness is called Wu Wei, which can be translated as "nothing extra." It is sometimes translated as "no-thing." "Nothing extra" means that we add no extra opinions, thoughts, beliefs and preconceived ideas to our direct experience of our essential nature (spirit). To live in the Tao is to live from our spirit, and the way to do this is by living in Wu Wei.

The Shen includes the Small Intestine and Heart's innate quality of living a natural life. The experiences of this fire system can include experiencing the unity of life, which can be a transcendental experience. With time, this awareness of the unity of life becomes normal and part of everyday life. Stagnation, blockages and repression of this aspect of life can manifest in intense outward expressions, which can be physical or emotional. For example, yelling, screaming, punching or emotional outbursts can occur at any time, reflecting the volatile and explosive nature of fire.

The Heart opens to the tongue. Shen imbalances can manifest in the way one speaks. The imbalance can include too much talking or the inability to express oneself clearly. A disconnect from spirit can occur, which can lead to a loss of passion for life. This type of separation can lead to bitterness (the taste and quality of the Heart).

Connecting to our Heart shen is an essential experience in many spiritual traditions. Practitioners of the healing arts can assist others in making this connection or realization; it is one of the most powerful and life-changing experiences for both the practitioner and the patient.

The Kidneys (Zhi)

The Kidneys house the zhi shen, which corresponds to Jing and genetics. The Kidneys and the Bladder are the water system. Ancestral medicine is one of the oldest sources of medicine in China. It originates in the Shang dynasty. During this time, the Chinese viewed the living and the deceased as existing simultaneously; most importantly, they influence each other. A modern interpretation of this ancestral influence is genetics. It can also include the culture, religion and beliefs of family, caretakers and those with an influence during early life. Transcending any unfavorable effects of those influences is essential to living a fulfilling life. If they are not transcended, they can lead to increased stagnation and rigidity. They can freeze a person.

Zhi relates to willpower. It includes the will and power to follow one's destiny. The Kidneys loathe cold, which can freeze water and change its essential nature of adaptability and flexibility. The Kidney acupuncture channel flows up the front of the body to the chest through the Heart area. This pathway is one example of zhi seeking shen—a person seeking their true nature. It is a built-in energetic system in each person. If there is an energy freezing or rigidity due to conditioning, we may not be able to have a full life. The freezing can change the flowing and adaptive nature of each person, possibly blocking awareness of his or her Shen.

A goal in life should be to allow expression of the issues related to the freezing of the zhi. Expression allows for freeing up stagnations and blockages. For example, if a person wanted to be an artist but did not pursue it, a part of them is suppressed or repressed. The suppression can lead to a deep polarity. If a person pursues artistic activities, it allows important qualities of the person to be experienced, allowing a free flow of energy. The expression is a type of letting go. Letting go can create awareness free of polarity, which can inspire and initiate change and transformation.

Chapter 11 of the *Tao Teh Ching* expresses this subtle truth:

Thirty spokes together make a wheel for a cart. It is the empty space in the center of the wheel which enables it to be used.

Mold clay in a vessel. It is the emptiness within that creates the usefulness of the vessel.

Cut out doors and windows in a house. It is the empty space inside that creates the usefulness of the house.

Thus, what we have may be something substantial, but its usefulness lies in the unoccupied, empty space.

The substance of your body is enlivened by maintaining the part of you that is unoccupied.[3]

The empty space in us is created when we let go of stagnations and blockages, allowing us to focus and recognize our present awareness (mindfulness of spirit). This awareness is the empty space described in Chapter 11 of the *Tao Teh Ching*. The empty space is a way of describing the most essential part of every person. The Chinese call this empty space Shen. Awareness of this empty space is Shen realization.

The zhi and Jing represent unlimited possibilities. In Chinese philosophy, it is called "chaos" or Wu Ji, which is a state or Qi field where anything is possible. And it is awareness or an openness that allows anything to manifest. No limits are placed on it. This space is inside each person. When we live from this space, there is no freezing or rigidity placed on the Kidneys, Jing and the zhi (the organ, substance and shen). If our ancestral influences (genes) or our family postnatal influences freeze or block our ability to be open to all possibilities, our Kidneys and zhi will be unfavorably affected, which will require

---

3   Ni, H.-C. (1979) *The Complete Works of Lao Tzu*. Chapter 25. Malibu, CA: The Shrine of the Eternal Breath of Tao.

freeing these blockages. Treatment and cultivation that frees one from the freezing can enable a person to live from their Shen, living in present awareness of spirit, one's true nature.

The Kidneys open to the ears. Zhi imbalances can manifest in hearing conditions—not only diminished hearing, but also not hearing or understanding what others are saying.

The Liver (Hun)

The Liver houses the hun, which corresponds to the ethereal shen. The Liver and Gallbladder are the wood system. The hun relates to the collective consciousness. It is the "we" aspect of consciousness or awareness. A person with a wood/hun imbalance can be driven by the need to be active in working with others for the benefit of the community, society or the collective; the person may be compensating for a lack in this area of their life. This activity or expression can include putting oneself in situations that allow concern for others to manifest, which helps raise awareness of this situation and the opportunity to learn about it and grow. If a person has been in an environment that blocks this expression, they may act in a way that is contrary to their desired behavior. If the person is not able to live in a natural way, a suppressed or repressed blockage is preventing this expression. This might be acting in a selfish way, which is the opposite of unity and community. A treatment plan for this person would be to unblock the areas of stagnation to allow expression related to the hun.

Balance is key in Chinese medicine. Our Shen temperament needs to be balanced. If one's expression is extreme, it is not balanced and can lead to pathological patterns. If hun qualities are expressed to an extreme, one can be too attached to the collective and other people, to the cost of one's own health and well-being. In a way, a person may be rejecting their life and taking on the extreme wood nature of rising and flying away, which can be an escape from their body or their life. Balanced activity is a key to creating an environment for all shen to be expressed in life.

The Liver and hun relate to planning and thinking about the future and how to achieve goals. If there is an extreme or imbalanced quality within these aspects of a person, we can consider it a hun imbalance and condition. Chinese medicine and nei dan practice can clear the blockages in the channels and the organs, and let a normal flow of energy through the Liver and the entire body. This normal flow of Qi, which includes the psycho-emotional condition, contributes to restoring balance.

The Liver opens to the eyes. Hun imbalances can manifest in seeing problems, diminished eyesight or lack of perception. This can also be a lack of insight or inner seeing, not just physical vision.

The Lungs (Po)

The Lungs house the po, which corresponds to the corporeal shen. The Lungs and the Large Intestine are the metal system. The po relates to the physical body. The correspondences include the senses, desires and pleasure. Imbalances in the po can manifest as over-attachments to those areas of life. The po can be expressed as selfishness. It's the "me, me, me" aspect of self. Selfishness and greediness can be part of a po disharmony.

The Large Intestine is the only primary channel that crosses the midline of the body. Some refer to it as the channel of polarity. A polarized po is a common condition in modern society. Loneliness is a common condition of the imbalanced po. Part of this comes from its ability to polarize itself, causing separation from others, society and life itself. Out of this polarity, isolation, separation and an intensified loneliness can occur. These imbalanced experiences and emotions can prompt a response to the polarization, which can initiate change. Loneliness and unhappiness can lead a person to seek another way to live and experience life; the driving force is the body's innate intelligence to seek balance. The nei dan practitioner can spend more time on the po correspondences to release the intensities of an imbalanced po.

The Lungs are connected to the nose. Breathing is a key to bringing the po into the present moment, freeing one from the polarity of the po. There is no polarity or separation in the present moment. Polarity only occurs in thoughts of the past or the future. Polarity creates separation, isolation and loneliness. Breathing practices, including Qi gong and Tai Chi Chuan, are traditional ways to regulate the breath, calm the po and promote balance.

The Spleen (Yi)

The Spleen houses the yi shen. The element of the Spleen and the Stomach is earth. The yi corresponds to intellect, thoughts,

concepts, ideas and beliefs. Grounding, organizing and diges-
tion are qualities of the earth, the Spleen and the Stomach.
The Spleen corresponds to the mouth, which processes food
and drink, and transforms them into nutritive substances. The
condition of the Spleen and the Stomach directly influences
that transformation process. Transforming food and drink
is the physical transformation. The earth organs—the Spleen
and Stomach—are also involved in the psycho-emotional transformation process. Similar to how food and drink go into the
mouth to be processed and transformed, all experiences in life
are processed by the yi. The yi organizes, categorizes, filters and
makes sense of our life experiences. In the same way that the
condition of the Spleen and the Stomach determines the quality
of the nutrition processed from digesting food, the condition
of the yi is instrumental in the processing of our experiences
in life, as well as our emotional well-being.

The condition of our yi, which includes the way we perceive, experience and process life, influences the hun, po, zhi
and shen. The yi includes our thinking and opinions about
people and life. If the yi is in an imbalanced or unhealthy
state, all five shen and their correspondences are influenced.
The yi, as the transformer, processes our experiences. The yi
includes the intellect and thoughts. When these qualities are
over-developed, the other aspects of our body, mind and spirit
become imbalanced. When the yi is imbalanced, we become
rigid and narrow, and respond to life in a conditioned way.
We often respond to life based on our past experiences. However, often the retroactive understanding is rooted in fear,

anger, misconceptions and prejudice; these influences create a conditioned response.

The yi is susceptible to fixed, rigid and repetitive patterns and reactions to life experiences. One reason is that the Spleen, and therefore the yi, has a function of holding. The Spleen organ holds blood in the vessels; the yi shen holds as well. It holds emotions and thoughts in the mind and in the blood. This holding function explains how the yi holds on to experiences and how we can live in these held experiences; this is living in the past.

The yi includes mindfulness. What we place attention on and retain in our mind is mindfulness. The yi can be overwhelmed by experiences, especially when we encounter them at a young age and are not yet capable of fully dealing with them. The yi can go into survival mode and create patterns of behavior that can become constitutional hyper-reactive ways of responding to life. These imprints need to be understood so that we can be released from their influence. When we do that, we can be open to the spontaneity of life. Becoming open to life as it is, not what it should be, not what it must be and not as we desire it to be, allows us to live from our Shen. Living from our Shen allows us to live in the present moment in a spontaneous way.

The yi can be imbalanced when one is too attached to thoughts and emotions. A person can become trapped in them. Then they are living primarily in past experiences. They can also be worrying about the future; in this case, they are living in the future. A person will tend to suffer from repetitive and obsessive thoughts and thinking due to the inability to let go.

Not being able to let go of the past or future prevents one from living in the present moment.

Feelings can be viewed as normal, natural aspects of life; they are spontaneous. An imbalanced yi can try to hold on to these feelings, trying to artificially retain something that should be experienced and allowed to leave, like the way the sun and the moon flow through endless cycles of waxing and waning. This trying creates a separation that blocks us from fully experiencing the present moment.

The imbalanced yi will hold and maintain past experiences, keeping them alive by continually thinking about them. Viewing these feelings as wei or superficial energetics is Yang. This energetic quality includes the natural flow of appearing and leaving. To keep these feelings alive takes Yin, which has the quality to store and maintain. The Spleen and the yi's Yin quality is blood. Through continual thinking about feelings or experiences, the Spleen's energetics transforms them into emotions, which are then stored in the blood. This process illustrates how we keep feelings alive beyond their usefulness. What we then hold is not the real experience; it is a thought or memory. This holding process becomes part of our conditioning, and eventually it can become part of the constitution. It can lead to the inability to live our lives in a naturally spontaneous way.

The yi corresponds to earth, which has the qualities of being rooted and grounded. The yi also includes the Stomach and Spleen's innate quality of being grounded in one's thoughts. But being stuck in one's thoughts can prevent a person from being open to new viewpoints, understandings, choices and actions.

This thought stagnation prevents us from letting go of the past, preventing the ability to experience life in a spontaneous way. The Spleen opens to the mouth. Yi imbalances can manifest in eating disorders because imbalances of the Spleen/Stomach and the yi/mouth can be expressed in the mouth and eating.

In my experience, the yi is the main cause of emotional conditions. It influences how the other shen respond to people and life. How the yi is involved in the creation of emotions is explained in the next chapter. Nei dan can have a profound influence on the yi, and, consequently, every aspect of our well-being.

Five Shen Group Dynamics

The five shen is a model that can become the basis of diagnosis and treatment plans. When the five shen correspondences become familiar, their imbalances become clear. The root of an imbalance can originate in a variety of sources, including prenatal and postnatal influences.

It is important to view the five shen as five aspects of one Shen (a person). Each of the five shen contains unique aspects of a person. And each shen shapes other shen in a way required for a person to be whole. The five-phases cycles illustrate important relationships within the five shen. Figure 2.2 depicts the five shen in circular formation. When the controlling (ko) cycle is in balance, it is a harmonizing force. When there is an imbalance, it can create unfavorable conditions; it can be over-acting. Each organ/shen contains an innate intelligence, which contains a message to be sent to its related shen (it provides an integral aspect of the functioning of its partner). The five-phases cycles are the patterns for these integral relationships.

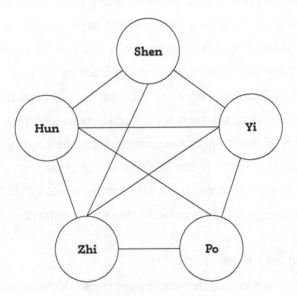

FIGURE 2.2 THE FIVE SHEN

The Shen and Po

The five shen (five phases) cycles contain a shaping or message-sharing function. For example, the Heart shen or fire has a controlling or shaping relationship with the Lungs and the po. The Heart shen sends its energy or message to the po. The message from the Heart shen to the Lung po is that we are essentially spirit. This realization guides the po spirit in its expression of the physical aspect of life. The po qualities are close to the physical body, the physical aspect of life. When it is imbalanced, it is susceptible to being more polarized, creating imbalances that can manifest as selfishness. This selfishness can include an unhealthy pursuit of one's own needs, desires and pleasures, often ignoring other people's needs. It's the Heart shen that expresses to the po its original nature, the yuan shen. The relationship is seen and practiced in the nei dan meditation. The balance of the two allows for the smooth expression of the po in life. This expression is guided by the Heart shen. When the shen and the po are in balance, this interaction and exchange is always occurring. When we create a life that maintains this relationship, our experience is a natural, spontaneous expression of spirit. It can be called living in the Tao or living in spirit. Spiritual traditions around the world call it Christ consciousness, Krishna consciousness or Buddha nature.

The Po and Hun

The po shen contains the innate intelligence of the importance of living in this world and living in our body, enjoying it and allowing full expression of our life in the here and now. The po sends this message to the hun spirit (metal controlling or shaping wood), which is the ethereal spirit. The hun includes the collective aspect of our life. This is the aspect of our life that we experience when we are attuned to the whole, part of a collective society and a unified universe. When the hun is imbalanced, it can include a denial of the physical body; this can be when a person pursues a spiritual direction in an attempt to deny the physical body and life. If there is a rejection of the physical body and life, a deep polarization can occur. The imbalanced hun can cause an individual to be too involved in society or assisting others to the detriment of their own health. One may believe it is of greater value to help others, but if it is a denial of a healthy enjoyment of their physical life and body, then it is a rejection of their physical needs and desires. This rejection can create a polarity and separation, which creates an imbalance not only of the po and hun but also of the other shen. The po–hun relationship includes the balanced relationship between self and others, and the individual and society.

The Hun and Yi

The hun contains the innate intelligence of the collective aspect of life. The hun sends this message to the yi, the Spleen's shen. This interaction is wood shaping or influencing earth. The yi contains our conceptual or intellectual capabilities. This is our ability to reason, be logical and organize and categorize; it includes intention (focus). The Spleen and the yi process not only food and drink but also our experiences of life. When the yi is imbalanced, it can lead to separation of oneself from other people and society, creating isolation and polarization.

Being too attached to thoughts and concepts turns a person's attention from real life, which creates a schism, because the body innately knows there is one reality. The reality is living in the present. Additionally, an imbalanced yi can manifest as obsessive and repetitive actions. These actions may be rooted in an extreme or distorted understanding or perception of experiences or thoughts. The hun can send its energy and message to the yi: the message is that we are part of the whole of life, not separate from it. Yi qualities are just one aspect of a person and not the primary aspect. The hun can help balance the yi to receive and process life in a clear, spontaneous way, and not in a conditioned, repetitive way.

The Yi and Zhi

The yi or earth shapes or sends a message to the zhi, the shen of the Kidneys. The zhi contains an innate intelligence of our unlimited nature, the capacity to become anything. This is called "chaos" in Taoist philosophy; it is our primordial nature. It is before thinking, before the dualistic categorization of all things in life. When the yi aspect of our life is over-developed, we become conditioned in how we respond to people, activities and situations. An imbalanced yi can have a significant influence on the zhi. It can overact on it, forcing it into a specific shape, which can prevent its natural free-flowing nature from being expressed.

The zhi contains willpower, the will and power to achieve goals and objectives. It is also the will and power to live the type of life we desire. One variation of this is the will and desire to seek our true nature, and then live from it. Zhi corresponds to water. Water's nature includes taking any form or shape; it is the flexibility to adapt to all situations. The zhi loathes cold. One reason for this is that cold freezes water, changing its innate nature of adaptability. The yi can help shape the zhi to accomplish goals and objectives. One way it does this is by applying focus on achieving or accomplishing.

The zhi needs some direction or focus; without that, it can spread itself around too much and not accomplish what it wants. The relationship between the yi and the zhi, earth and water, and the prenatal and postnatal, can be found in many aspects of Chinese medicine.

A balanced yi provides a favorable focus and intention that allows the zhi to unfold in a healthy way. If the yi is imbalanced, it can cause rigid thinking and actions, and can create repetitive and obsessive activities. The zhi needs the yi to have an openness to receive and experience life. Openness allows the zhi to maintain the ability to be flexible and adaptive. The zhi needs this to allow its natural unfolding and the fulfillment of one's destiny of spiritual realization.

The Zhi and Shen

The zhi or water shapes and sends its energy to the Heart shen. This relationship is the classic Chinese model of Yin–Yang, water–fire, Shao Yin and Jing–Shen. This relationship can be viewed as the zhi's capacity to become anything. There is a clear direction within all these possibilities: it is Jing seeking Shen, the zhi seeking the Heart shen. The Kidneys' acupuncture pathway flows past the Heart area; it is the zhi seeking the shen. These relationships are the innate structure within the body to connect to spirit.

The Heart shen contains our true nature. Some traditions view realization of this aspect of our nature as the primary goal or purpose of life, the common destiny among all people. This realization provides the opportunity to live from this awareness. Jing seeking Shen can be viewed as our quest in life. The models of Jing–Shen, water–fire and Yin–Yang, along with the trajectory connections between the Kidneys and Heart, show the inner energetic system reflecting this quest.

Table 2.1 summarizes fundamental information about the five shen. This information can be used to make a five shen diagnosis and to determine which shen, organs and emotions to focus on in nei dan practice.

Table 2.1 Five shen and correspondences

Zhi Water	Kidneys Bladder	Lineage, genetics, willpower, reproduction, destiny, unlimited possibilities, destiny code, the will to live your destiny
Hun Wood	Liver Gallbladder	Collective, intelligence, growth, cultivation, direction Ethereal, planning, decision making, judgments
Shen Fire	Heart Small Intestine	Spirit, consciousness, quest, guidance, intuition, yuan shen, true nature, wisdom, true spirit
Yi Earth	Spleen Stomach	Concepts, thoughts, intellect, grounding, rooting, practical, digesting life experiences, organizing, holding emotions/thoughts/blood, mindfulness, polarity, separation
Po Metal	Lungs Large Intestine	Physical body, physical desires, sensitivity to emotions, selfishness, isolation, inability to forgive

The five shen information presented in this chapter is found in the healing sounds, the inner-smile and the five shen nei dan practices. When there are imbalances related to a five shen system, spend more time cultivating that system. The information in this chapter and in following chapters provides an effective framework for self-healing and cultivation.

CHAPTER 3

Emotions

The early practitioners of Chinese medicine had a profound understanding of how the psycho-emotional condition of a person can influence that person's life. They understood the inseparable relationship between the physical body and emotions. The Han dynasty classic, the *Nei Jing*, presents the six exogenous pathogens (wind, cold, damp, heat, summer heat and dryness) and the seven emotions as major causes of illness. The seven emotions are anger, joy (too much joy), sadness, grief, pensiveness, fear and fright. The practitioners perceived that the emotions and the organs (physical body) influence each other. The understanding of this symbiotic relationship is the basis of holistic healing and Chinese medicine.

The ancient healers differentiated natural virtues and emotions. Natural virtues occur when we live in a natural and spontaneous way. The natural virtues are the fundamental qualities of a person. In the Taoist tradition of Lao Zi, Wu Wei (nothing extra) is the name given to the natural and spontaneous way of living life. The Taoists experienced how living in Wu Wei naturally attuned a person to their Shen and allowed their life to be an expression of it. The natural expression includes living in balance. Balance encompasses a range, not a point. Within this view of balance is the ability to respond to situations in an appropriate way, which at times can create an imbalance, following which one naturally adjusts back to a balanced state. The capacity for adjusting is the key. If a person has clarity about who they are—in this case, their Shen (Shen is the natural self)—they are able to deal with difficulties and challenges in life from their Shen; if they are thrown off balance, they will realign to their natural self quickly. The duration of this realigning process varies among people. With a clear understanding of what we are (Shen), the duration decreases as we begin to realize the attachment is to a false identity and we realize that quicker and quicker. Being free from this veil of false identity allows awareness of Shen, and the opportunity to be a living expression of Shen in normal, everyday life. A common way to describe this is "present awareness." In my experience, being mindful of present awareness is living in Wu Wei, living in the Tao.

What Are Emotions?

From a Taoist psychological viewpoint, imbalanced emotions can be described as an experience that creates a polarity and a psycho-emotional imbalance strong enough that a person does not live from balance and naturalness. Emotions are a normal part of life. A goal for healthy living is to be able to let them go and not retain them for longer than a normal time frame. A normal time frame can vary for each person. Most spiritual traditions include forgiveness and unconditional love as part of their value system; both are a way of letting go. A primary aspect of nei dan practice is learning to let go of emotions and imbalanced experiences, and to attune to the present moment. Within that present awareness is living in the spontaneity of life, not conditioning of the past and thoughts of the future. The ancient healers created numerous ways that can help to let go of experiences and emotions that create imbalances. Qi gong, meditation, dance, reading, chanting, herbal medicine, acupuncture and *I Ching* and *Tao Teh Ching* philosophy are some of the methods and philosophies that comprise cultivation practices for understanding life stresses and the imbalances they can create.

Emotions not properly processed are a major cause of illness and changes in the disposition of a person. As a major cause of imbalance, it is necessary to understand what they are, how they are formed and how they can be treated. Emotions have a strong effect on the Heart and the Shen. In Chinese medicine, the Heart is the residence of the Shen. Chapter 71 of the *Ling Shu*, "The Evil Guest," presents this relationship:

> Qi Bo said, "The heart is the grand master of the five organs and the six bowels. The heart is the shelter of seminal essence and spirit. The organs are solid. Evil must not appear. If it appears it causes injury to the heart and the spirit to depart, which causes death."[1]

---

1   Wu, J. (2002) *Ling Shu or The Spiritual Pivot.* Chapter 71. Honolulu, HI: University of Hawai'i Press.

This *Ling Shu* reference can be interpreted as saying that the Heart is the center of importance and influence of the internal organs and their correspondences. These correspondences include the natural virtues and emotions. Evil pathogenic factors (exogenous and endogenous pathogenic factors) must not enter the Heart because if the Heart is injured, then the internal organs, Jing and the Shen will be harmed. If the Heart is injured, the spirit will depart, and this will cause death. "Death" can also mean that a person feels separate, alone, lost and isolated (socially isolated). In this instance, the injured Heart causes polarity and a feeling of separation. The polarity, separation, isolation and the feeling of being lost influence the entire person. The seminal essence is Jing, and it represents both the physical body and the psycho-emotional condition generated by life experiences. These experiences are held in the body (Jing), creating imprints and conditioning; this experiential conditioning is a normal process. It is the over-attachment to these life experiences that can harm the balance within you (the five shen and Shen awareness). Attachment to the yi (the imbalances) is part of this conditioning; attachment is part of the holding. If the Heart and Shen are harmed, the body and mind are affected. Having a healthy Heart and Shen is essential for having a healthy life. The *Ling Shu* passage quoted above reminds us of this reality of life.

The *Su Wen* and the *Ling Shu* describe how pathogens can transfer throughout the body. The six exogenous pathogenic factors can be transferred from the superficial levels to the deeper levels of the body. The seven emotions (emotional Qi) can be transferred into the blood, muscles, acupuncture channels and internal organs. They can also enter the deep Jing levels to become part of the constitution. This transfer is part of the process by which emotions can influence the entire body and how they are held in the body. The yi plays a critical role in holding emotions in the body.

How Emotions Are Formed

Human life includes a wide range of experiences. As we interact in life and accumulate experiences, we process them. The processing of experiences includes making sense of them, which contributes to the formation of the ego. The ego is part of the yi. The choices we make in our daily life are influenced by the yi. All being well, a nurturing, supporting and loving environment is provided during early childhood to allow natural and healthy interactions for development of the yi. When that supportive environment does not exist, a process of emotional pathology can occur. The repetitive influences of an unhealthy environment create an emotionally polarizing type of conditioning and a powerfully negative influence on a person. The ancient healers understood this process and developed ways to assist a person in changing the effects of it. Part of this change involves understanding how imbalanced emotions are formed.

The Formation of the Yi

The formation of the yi involves life interactions, our responses
to them and how they influence our life. If there is a loving and
encouraging environment, a child is influenced by it. How does
this influence occur? It is by daily exposure that influences all
the interwoven layers of a person: the physical, mental/emo-
tional and the spiritual. A continual healthy influence can form
a healthy yi that enters the deep level in a person (Jing level),
which then becomes the constitution and the basic aspect of
a person. If, by contrast, a child is in an environment that is
continually full of anger, fear, sadness, depression and worry,
they continually process those negative feelings which become
part of the child's constitution and everyday nature. When a
child is continually exposed to either of these favorable or unfavorable environments, the experiences become part of the yi.
An analogy would be how the quality of the food and fluids we
consume each day influences our body and mind. Years and
decades of a certain nutritional quality profoundly influence
a person. If the nutritional quality is good, there is a good
influence. If it is not good, there is an unfavorable influence
on health. This process works the same way in the emotional
environment (the yi digesting and processing life experiences).
We can view emotions as emotionally charged Qi, and this Qi is
continually influencing Jing–Qi–Shen (body–mind–spirit).

When each person is living a natural and spontaneous life,
their life is expressed in that way, naturally and spontaneously;
what is expressed in that naturalness is called natural virtues.
When we live from a conditioned response, we are living from

deep, old patterns of our prior experiences. We are not living in the present but from memories of the past or dreams of the future. Emotions can become the basis of conditioned responses to life. For example, when a child is around an angry person every day, most likely they are being influenced by that emotion. They can then express anger in the way they act, regardless of whether it is an appropriate response to a situation. The person can also repress anger, causing the anger Qi to flow deeper in the channel system, the internal organs and Jing. This is an example of how the emotion is internalized. This can cause a powerful effect on the Liver and Gallbladder organs, their correspondences and their functioning. Because the five phases are really one integrated whole, they influence others in the whole. The anger (Liver) can influence any of the other organs/shen. In this particular example, the influence will most likely be unfavorable. For example, the Liver hun can influence its child, the Heart shen; its grandchild, the Spleen yi; the grandparent, the Lung po; and its parent, the Kidney zhi.

Chapter 62 of the *Su Wen*, "Regulation of the Channels," says the following about the five shen:

The five types of excess and deficiency are borne from the five zang organs. For example, the heart houses the shen or spirit; the lungs house the Qi; the liver accommodates the blood; the spleen houses the form and flesh; and the kidneys house the zhi, or will. They must all function together as the zhi and the shen are functioning in concert psychically, connecting with the bones and marrow within and forming the shape of the body without. This creates an entire functioning being and is the makeup of the human body. Within the five zang, communication occurs via pathways or channels, which transport Qi and blood. When the Qi and blood are not regulated, illness occurs. Diagnosis and treatment depend on channels and pathways.[2]

This passage from the *Su Wen* describes how the proper functioning of the five zang organs and the circulation of Qi and blood are necessary for health. Emotions can unfavorably influence both of those functions, causing, in turn, an unfavorable effect on the Shen. Maintaining a healthy emotional condition is essential for health and vitality.

A key to health, vitality and well-being is a healthy circulation of Qi and blood throughout the body. Qi comprises everything in life; therefore, it encompasses feelings, emotions and experiences. If the emotions create a stagnation and blockage, they can create illness of the body–mind–spirit (Jing–Qi–Shen). Practitioners should be able to determine where these stagnations exist. The framework for determining where stagnation exists can found in the channel system. Identifying the channels involved provides the basis for a targeted treatment. Emotional stagnations can influence all the channel systems and the internal organs. Understanding the process of how the environment and lifestyle influence a person offers a way to reverse the impact of the influence. Chinese medicine, nei dan, medical Qi gong and

2   Ni, M. (1995) *The Yellow Emperor's Classic of Medicine: A New Translation of NeiJing Suwen with Commentary*. Boston, MA: Shambhala.

lifestyle guidance, along with the appropriate allopathic medical care, can assist a person in changing their life.

Chinese Medical Theory of Blood and Emotions
The Creation of Blood

In Chinese medicine, food and fluids are transformed and transported in the Spleen and the Stomach. One transformation of these substances is into gu Qi (nutrient Qi), which is transported to the Lungs and the Heart to eventually create blood. The Heart then circulates the blood throughout the body. The Spleen assists the Heart in the circulation of blood by holding it in the blood vessels. The focus in this section is the relationship between the Spleen and the Heart; other organs are involved in the creation of blood, but their relationships are not discussed in this chapter.

Creating, circulating and holding blood in the blood vessels are the three main functions of the Spleen and the Heart. Understanding these functions contributes to understanding the formation and holding of emotions in the body, which reveals a way nei dan is used to undo the holding of emotions.

The Shen and Blood

In Chinese medicine, the Heart houses the Shen, and the Shen's qualities include our emotional well-being. The Heart is also involved in the creation and circulation of blood. Those three roles of the Heart—housing the Shen and making and circulating blood—link the Heart, the Shen, emotions and blood. This dynamic explains one aspect of why the Shen and emotions are stored in the blood.

The Spleen and Blood

The Spleen works with the Heart to make and circulate blood. The Spleen creates gu Qi from food and fluids, and sends it to the Lungs and the Heart to make blood. The Spleen's energetics includes holding blood in the vessels. When it does not hold blood in the vessels, there can be reckless bleeding. This is the Spleen's physical function. There is also a psycho-emotional holding. The yi holds thoughts, feelings, emotions and experiences in the blood. When the yi does not hold and release in a balanced way, it can cause reckless mental activity. When the yi holds too much, there can be repetitive and possibly obsessive thinking.

The Yi and the Ego

The Spleen holds physical substances, thoughts and emotions. The yi, the Spleen's shen, contains our intellectual, conceptual and thinking qualities; it also includes our ego. The formation of our ego—opinions, preferences and emotional attachments— is part of the yi. While the Spleen holds blood in the vessels, the yi holds thoughts, feelings and emotions in the blood. The Spleen holds all of its correspondences. This physical and psycho-emotional function explains the mechanism for how the Spleen and thoughts, feelings and emotions are stored in the blood.

When we do not let go of emotions (experiences), the body can respond in several ways. First, emotions are a form of Qi. Qi is Yang compared with blood, which is Yin. The emotion (Yang) is stored in a Yin substance, blood. When there is repetitive thinking, the body believes the person wants to keep these thoughts and the feelings associated with them. The Heart and the Spleen will hold them in the blood, the Yin substance related to these organs. The body will desire to hold the experiences. This is due to the yi function of holding. When we have an experience and want to maintain it and relive it, or when we have trauma and can't let go of it, all of the five shen and the Shen can be influenced as a result of the yi becoming overly active in its inability to let go of the experience and the emotion(s). In other words, the yi holds on to the experiences and continually relives them; this is because of the holding function. We then live from this past experience or from a desire for something to manifest in the future. This creates a pattern or imprint that is repeated until the experience is let go and the natural virtues within a person can be expressed.

How Emotions Can Influence a Person

Each day and night, blood circulates throughout the entire body. During this circulation, the qualities in the blood, which include emotions, continually influence a person. Initially, this influence is at a superficial level, but if the circulation of emotional Qi continues, it will eventually enter the deeper levels of a person. The influence flows from the wei level to the yuan level (superficial to deep levels). Trauma can quickly enter the yuan level. This process of trauma being quickly absorbed indicates how important it is to let go of emotions to maintain a healthy psycho-emotional condition. The *Su Wen* and the *Ling Shu* describe numerous ways in which pathogens can transfer through the body. For example, in Chapter 63 of the *Su Wen*, "Acupuncturing the Superficial Luo," pathogens in the luo collaterals can transfer first to the main channels and then to the internal organs. Also, the Ying Qi cycle (daily clock), which is described in Chapter 16 of the *Ling Shu*, "Nourishing Qi," suggests that postnatal pathogens can move through the body from the Lungs to the Liver. In this cycle, not only does the cycle flow back to the Lungs from the Liver to repeat an endless process through the twelve channels, the internal organs and the five shen, but a branch also flows to the Du and Ren channels. This connection from the main channels to the Eight Extraordinary Channels is a reminder that if we do not resolve issues in our daily life, they can move deeper into the constitutional level.

A Process for Change

The process of emotionally charged blood circulating throughout the body influences the three treasures: Jing, Qi and Shen. It can also explain a process whereby natural virtues can influence our well-being and health. Each person can consciously determine what flows in that cycle—natural virtues can be guided into that process to rejuvenate the body. With Qi gong, meditation, prayer, reading, etc., we can fill the yi with the natural virtues and enlightening experiences. With continual practice (cultivation), the yi holds the natural virtues in thoughts (through mindfulness) and eventually in our blood. These natural experiences and virtues will circulate throughout the entire body to nourish it.

The yi is the filtering mechanism of life experiences (Figure 3.1). If we change the yi, we change the way we experience life. Nei dan inner meditation is a method to let go emotionally charged Qi and the psycho-emotional condition it creates. The effects will flow from the wei level to the yuan level of a person (from superficial to deep). This is a way to change our life and attune to our spirit. The six healing sounds is a powerful way to begin that process; it begins the process of letting go and focusing attention on areas of the body.

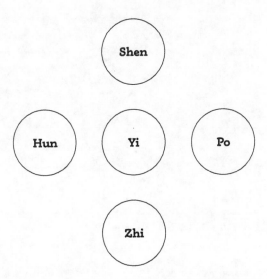

FIGURE 3.1 THE YI SHEN AS THE CENTER AND TRANSFORMER

CHAPTER 4

The Healing Sounds Nei Dan

Natural healing practices are a significant contribution from Chinese culture. One of the oldest and most important natural healing practices is Qi gong (dao yin). A unique aspect of Qi gong is that it can be incorporated into daily life without having to visit a practitioner; it can be practiced in the comfort of a home, office, backyard or park. Daily practice influences health, vitality and well-being.

Qi gong is a general term that includes a wide range of postures, movements, breath and sound practice. Medical Qi gong is targeted to treat specific conditions. This natural healing system includes the principles of Chinese medicine. The healing sounds are a medical Qi gong practice.

The ancient Chinese perceived that humanity and nature are inseparable. From observing life, they developed models that expressed the relationships they saw in it. The models include Yin–Yang, Tai Chi and the five phases (five elements). All of life can be viewed in these three flows or patterns. One of the most insightful discoveries of the ancient Chinese was that these models are "systems of correspondences" (relationships between two or more things). The ability to perceive and predict how one correspondence can influence others is the essence of Chinese medicine. Medical Qi gong uses this model as a guide to influence correspondences within the body to obtain health and vitality. The healing sounds Qi gong presented in this chapter includes important correspondences of the internal organs and the five shen (five spirits).

Chapter 5 of the classic Chinese medical book the *Nei Jing Su Wen*, "The Manifestation of Yin and Yang from the Macrocosm to the Microcosm," introduces the five shen. The five shen can be viewed as five aspects of a person. They are stored or housed in the Yin organs and their influence extends throughout the body. Each of the five shen corresponds with one of the five phases (five elements):

- the hun is housed in the Liver, which is wood

- the shen is housed in the Heart, which is fire

- the yi is housed in the Spleen, which is earth

- the po is housed in the Lungs, which is metal

- the zhi is housed in the Kidneys, which is water.

Systems of correspondences include the relationship between organs, shen and emotions. This model includes the ability to influence one correspondence by influencing another. For instance, if the po shen is imbalanced and a person is suffering from sadness, treating the Lungs can influence this condition. Performing the Lungs healing sounds can treat the Lungs, po shen and the corresponding emotions.

Emotions are Qi, and the healing sounds have a powerful influence on Qi and emotions. When emotions are imbalanced, they can alter the way Qi flows. Emotions not only influence their own organ's Qi flow; they can alter the Qi of related organs in their five phases and Chinese medical relationships. For instance, if a person suffers from anger, the Liver can overact on earth and cause the Spleen to suffer from worry, its corresponding emotion. When the Liver overacts on the Spleen, worry can cause Qi to be stagnant and not flow upward, preventing the development of Qi and blood in the Lungs and the Heart. Understanding that emotions are Qi allows the practitioner to use numerous methods (including the healing sounds) to balance Qi and emotions.

Each of the five phases has a variety of correspondences. Some of the major correspondences are colors, emotions, organs, sensory organs, shen, sounds and shapes. Table 4.1 contains this information.

Table 4.1 The five-phases correspondences

	Wood	Fire	Earth	Metal	Water
Color	Green	Red	Yellow Gold	White Gold Silver	Blue-green Black
Direction	East	South	Center	West	North
Season	Spring	Summer	Indian summer	Fall	Winter
Yin organs	Liver	Heart	Spleen	Lungs	Kidneys
Yang organs	Gallbladder	Small Intestine	Stomach	Large Intestine	Bladder
Sense organs	Eyes	Tongue	Mouth	Nose	Ears
Emotions	Kindness Anger Irritability Frustration	Joy Love Hastiness Impatience Arrogance	Openness Receptiveness Pensiveness Worry Lamenting	Courage Sadness Loneliness Depression Grief Sorrow	Gentleness Fear Paranoia
Spirit	Hun	Shen	Yi	Po	Zhi
Sounds	Shhhh	Hawww	Hoooo	Sssss	Chuiii (the sound of a wave)
Shape	Rod	Triangle	Rectangle	Sphere Round	Cascading downward

Medical Qi gong includes one or more of the five-phases corre-spondences. The correspondences are included in Qi gong to stimulate and influence areas of the body, mind and spirit. One of the oldest and most popular medical Qi gong practices is the six healing sounds. The healing sounds are an ancient practice. Tao HongJing (AD 451–536) is one of the most famous Chinese medical doctors, Qi gong and nei gong practitioners, herbalists and San Qing Taoists in Chinese history. He promoted the heal-ing sounds as a medical Qi gong practice. Most Qi gong forms have many variations; the healing sounds also have numerous versions. All traditions have a sound, and some include pos-tures or shapes that reflect the five phases. There are forms that also include a posture, color and emotions. The healing sounds that contain all of those five-phases correspondences are a powerful medical Qi gong and an effective emotional transformational medical Qi gong.

The Basics of Medical Qi Gong

The basic goal of the healing sounds is to influence an organ, its channel and its correspondences by applying the three adjust-ments of medical Qi gong:

1. posture

2. breath

3. intention.

From a traditional Chinese medical viewpoint, medical Qi gong can clear heat or wind and break through Qi and blood stagnation. From a psycho-emotional viewpoint, the healing sounds can release unfavorable emotional Qi and allow reconnecting to the natural virtues. From a spiritual viewpoint, the healing sounds attune a person to the five shen. Attuning to the five shen (the five aspects of consciousness), allows a person to unite their yi (their attention, mindfulness) with their Qi and body as one integrated whole, allowing the natural expression of harmony and balance to occur. From a shamanic viewpoint, the Wu (healers) of ancient China used Qi gong to unite with the spirits of heaven, integrating heaven and earth.

Medical Qi gong should contain the three adjustments: posture, breath and intention. The following outlines the basic practice for the healing sounds. See the pictures below illustrating the postures.

1. Begin the healing sounds by taking a long, gentle, deep breath from the lower dan tian (the lower abdomen).

2. As you inhale, move your arms up the body into the proper position and then make the sound while exhaling.

3. Exhaling should be slow, gentle and as long as possible. Keep the body relaxed when doing this Qi gong. The eyes are open during exhaling.

4. When you finish exhaling, slowly and gently move your hands over the organ to which the sound corresponds;

the palms should face the body. The eyes are closed. You can also place your hands on your knees as well (see the pictures for each sound).

5. Move the tip of your tongue to your palate, behind your teeth; this enhances the natural flow and connection of Qi in the Du and Ren channels, two of the Eight Extraordinary Channels that flow up the back and down the front of the body (see Chapter 6).

6. Smile, and place your mind's attention in the organs to which the healing sounds are related; this guides Qi into the organs, energizing and rejuvenating them. Additionally, the well, spring and stream points (three of the five transporting acupuncture points) are on the hands, and they are among the most energetically powerful points on the body. Placing the hands over an organ transfers Qi to the organ to energize and rejuvenate it.

7. Keep your mind's attention (yi) in the organ as you inhale and exhale. Inhaling guides Qi into the organ, and exhaling with your yi in the organ keeps it there, reinforcing and energizing it.

8. Exhaling is the Yang stage; it releases excesses and stagnations and is a reducing method. The eyes are open during the Yang stage, the exhale.

9. The rest, or Yin stage, of the practice is a reinforcing method. The eyes are closed during the Yin stage when

there is normal breathing with the hands covering the organ.

The Healing Sounds Practice

There are two major aspects to the healing sounds practice. The first is to release unfavorable emotionally charged Qi and excesses (including gas, heat, fire, cold, wind, Qi and blood stagnations); that is a powerful medical Qi gong. The second aspect is to allow the natural virtue of the organ and shen to manifest. Releasing unfavorable emotional Qi and excess creates space for the natural virtues to be felt and expressed. With continual practice, these qualities will enter and permeate the body, nourishing it with natural and favorable virtues. This process allows us to manage our emotional condition, as well as providing the opportunity to take action to change and transform our life.

Medical Aspects of Respiration

Exhaling is the reducing method. It releases unfavorable emotions. It can also release pathogenic factors—for instance, wind, heat, fire, damp, phlegm and cold. The releasing or clearing process can assist in creating the smooth flow of Qi in the channels and the organs. Exhaling also cools the body.

The Rest Period

The rest period is the reinforcing method. When we place our hands over an organ, Qi flows there. The Qi nourishes and reinforces the organ. This is a rejuvenation practice.

Medical Prescription

When practicing the healing sounds for medical purposes, a medical prescription should be recommended that can be once a day or more, and a particular organ sound can be done three, six or nine times or more. To reduce or sedate, make the sound loudly. To reinforce, make the sound sub-vocally. As a maintenance practice, make a very low sound. The healing sounds are generally practiced once a day.

The Three Adjustments

The three adjustments are posture, intention and breath. Each of those adjustments enhances the healing sounds Qi gong practice. A synergy occurs when two or three of them are included in the practice. The healing sounds presented in this book include the three adjustments.

The Three Layers of Medical Qi Gong

The healing sounds have three layers. You decide to use one or more layers in your practice.

Layer 1: Smiling into the organ.

Layer 2: See the corresponding color of the organ.

Layer 3: Repeat the name of the natural virtues of the organ/shen.

- When exhaling you can just exhale or include the name and feeling of the corresponding emotions.

- In the rest stage, you can smile into the organs. You can also see the color of the organs. And you can repeat the name of the natural virtues of the corresponding organs.

- It's your choice how to use these layers based on what brings the best results. You can use one of them or combine two or include all three of them. The decision should be based on what you need at any given time. Be flexible in your choice.

It is traditional to repeat the sound three times. During each season, it is common to repeat the sound for the season six times. For example, during the fall perform the Lung and Large Intestine sound six times; we can be more influenced by the seasonal influence.

How to Practice the Healing Sounds
The Lungs and Large Intestine Healing Sound

The Lungs and Large Intestine are the metal phase and correspond to the po shen. The color is white, gold and silver. The sound is a hissing sound: "*sssss*." It is like the noise of a punctured tire. The Lung and Large Intestine's unfavorable emotions are sadness, depression, grief, loneliness and sorrow. Imbalances of the po include feelings of isolation and the inability to forgive. The favorable virtue is courage. The shape is sphere and round; therefore, we take a sphere or round-shaped position in this Qi gong. All of these correspondences are included in this medical Qi gong practice.

The three adjustments for the Lung and Large Intestine healing sound:

Posture: A sphere or round shape. Notice that the arms in this posture are in a sphere or round shape; see Figure 4.1.

Intention: During the exhale, release the unfavorable emotions from the Lungs and Large Intestine; in the rest stage, focus on the favorable one.

Breath: A long inhale to begin, and a long exhale when making the sound. In the rest stage, focus your attention/yi in the Lungs and the Large Intestine, and breathe naturally.

Begin with the hands on the knees, open the eyes and inhale as you move into the posture. After a slow, full inhale, make the Lung and Large Intestine sounds, exhaling slowly. After a full exhale, bring the arms down and cover your Lungs with your hands or bring to the beginning position. Close the eyes, place your tongue up to the palate, smile and breathe into the Lungs. The breath is gentle and from your lower abdomen, the lower dan tian.

FIGURE 4.1 THE LUNG AND LARGE INTESTINE HEALING SOUND

The Kidney and Bladder Healing Sound

The Kidney and Bladder correspond to the zhi shen, and to fear and paranoia as well as gentleness. During the exhale, release fear; during the rest period, allow gentleness to manifest. The zhi reflects our willpower and the will to live the type of life we desire. It includes the will to seek and understand our true nature (Shen realization). The Kidney acupuncture channel has

an internal pathway that flows to the Heart; this is the Kidney
zhi seeking the Heart shen.

The basic nature of water is to be fluid and adaptive, to
be able to adjust to any situation. When a person is frozen in
life, they become locked and rigid. If the zhi is frozen, fear can
manifest; it includes the fear of being trapped and limited.
It's a fear that prevents one from changing, from attempting
and accomplishing the things that comprise their most innate
purpose in life: to live from the Heart shen. The Kidney and
Bladder healing sound can release fear and the coldness that
can manifest from being frozen in life.

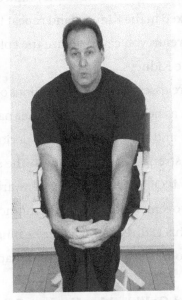

FIGURE 4.2 THE KIDNEY AND BLADDER HEALING SOUND

The Kidneys correspond to the back and the spine. Begin by
sitting in a chair with your back straight, inhale and slowly lean

forward, rounding your back and clasping your hands around your knees (see Figure 4.2). Exhale to the sound of a wave, just like the sound of a wave you hear at the beach: "*chuiii*." Make the sound based on your real-life understanding of the sound of a wave, not reading a word, which often does not provide an accurate guide. It should be a long, gentle exhale. While exhaling, you can just make the wave sound, or repeat the word "fear" to release any fear that may exist. When the breath has been fully exhaled, slowly inhale as you move back to the starting position. Sit with your hands on your knees or cover your Kidneys with your hands, and place your mind's attention/yi in the Kidneys. Breathe into the Kidneys and exhale into them, keep your yi fixed in the Kidneys and repeat the word "gentleness." If you prefer, you can visualize the color blue-green in and around the Kidneys.

The exhale releases the negative emotions of the Kidneys and the zhi, as well as heat, gas, cold and other pathogenic factors in the channel and the organ. The rest period is the reinforcing stage and strengthens the Kidneys. The shape of water is cascading. In this Qi gong, we move downward and forward—a cascade-like movement. The rounding of the back stimulates the Kidneys. This Kidney and Bladder healing sound practice combines the sound, emotions, color and shape of water.

The Liver and Gallbladder Healing Sound

The Liver and Gallbladder correspond to the hun. An imbalanced hun can be expressed as anger, irritability, frustration and a lack of direction. The hun also represents the aspect of our life that allows us to perceive the collective nature of all of humanity and nature. It perceives the unity and the inseparable nature of our life. Wood corresponds to the Liver, and when it is imbalanced, its energy can rise, float upward and float away. From a psychological viewpoint, this can mean a person tries to leave their everyday life, escape or lift up and away from it. This can include denying their physical body, or it can mean not wanting to interact with people. This leaving can be justified by attempting to be spiritual, being above the physical. Leaving this world is a rejection of the inseparable nature of life, the intrinsic nature of the hun. Its imbalance includes not maintaining its essential quality: the unity of humanity and life. This essential nature includes living from the unity of body, mind and spirit.

The Liver and Gallbladder healing sound is "shhhh." The breathing method for the healing sounds is a long inhale from the lower dan tian, and a long exhale when making the sound. The eyes should be open during the inhalation and the exhalation. Wood is rod-shaped and extends upward. During the sound, we assume a rod shape and extend upward. Begin with your hands on your knees, inhale slowly and deeply, lift your hands up in front of your body, clasp your fingers and extend your hands above your head (see Figure 4.3). Extend your arms about 95 percent and lean a little to the left, which creates a stretch on your right side and the Liver. Exhale to the "shhhh" sound (as you would "shhhh" a child to be quiet). It should be a long, gentle exhale. You can just make the sound, or you can repeat the name of the emotion for the Liver if the emotion is imbalanced, which can be anger, irritability or frustration.

If there is an intensity of the emotion(s), make the sound loudly. If the healing sounds are practiced as a daily wellness Qi gong, make the sound softly.

The rest period is as important as making the sound. When the sound is completed, lower your hands alongside your body and bring your hands near your knees (you can also place your hands over the Liver), close your eyes, place your tongue on the palate behind your teeth and focus your yi/attention in your Liver. Close your eyes (always close your eyes in the rest stage) and smile into your Liver. If you prefer, repeat the word "kindness" as you smile into the Liver. Exhaling and making the sound is the reducing (releasing) stage. The reinforcing stage is when you smile into the organ.

FIGURE 4.3 THE LIVER AND GALLBLADDER HEALING SOUND

The Heart and Small Intestine Healing Sound

The Heart and Small Intestine correspond to the Heart shen. The color of the Heart is red, its shape is a triangle, the direction is south, the planet is Mars, the taste is bitter, and the element is fire. The sound is "*hawww.*"

The Heart and Small Intestine healing sound has a strong influence on emotions and the Shen. It is essential to clear heat from the Heart and any unfavorable Qi and emotions from influencing it. The Heart and Small Intestine healing sound is a practical and effective way to harmonize the Heart and allow the virtues of joy and love to be naturally expressed in daily life.

FIGURE 4.4 THE HEART AND SMALL INTESTINE HEALING SOUND

The Inhale

Take a long, slow, gentle inhale from your lower dan tian, which includes your lower belly. As you inhale, bring your hands up in a big circle from the sides of the body into a praying posture in front of your body (see Figure 4.4).

The Exhale

Perform a long, slow exhale, making the "*hawww*" sound. Extend your arms out to the side of the body and repeat one or more of the following words: "hastiness," "impatience," "arrogance," "cruelty," "hatred." Release any of these emotions that exist. You can also just make the sound. Stay relaxed while inhaling and exhaling. Do not create any tension in your body during this Qi gong. When you have finished exhaling, cover your Heart with your hands. Place your intention in your Heart and smile. If you prefer, repeat "joy" and "love" silently to yourself as you smile into your Heart. Continue smiling to the Heart and Small Intestine for a few minutes until you feel joy and love.

The Spleen and Stomach Healing Sound

In five phases and five shen theory, the earth phase and the yi shen are in the center of the five phases. This center position indicates how earth influences all the five phases and how its condition influences all four of the other phases.

- The yi shen is our conceptual mind, our ability to think and organize thoughts. The Spleen yi relates to the mouth.

- The Kidney zhi is our will and hearing.

- The Liver hun represents the ethereal and our ability to understand the collective nature of our life and seeing (eyesight).

- The Heart shen represents our essential nature, our purpose, and relates to the tongue and speech.

- The Lung po represents the corporeal and the physical body, the nose, breathing and smell.

In the same way that the Spleen and Stomach are the origin of postnatal essences (they transform and transport the nutrients from food and drink throughout the body), the yi digests, transforms and processes all experiences in our life. All food and drink must go through the mouth; all processing of experiences goes through the yi. The yi transfers these experiences to the other four shen and their corresponding sensory organs. Figure 4.5 illustrates the five shen and the sensory organs. The healing sounds are a way to change the conditioning and patterns formed by the yi.

FIGURE 4.5 THE FIVE SHEN AND THE SENSORY ORGANS

The earth is a transforming phase; it receives and processes. The yi is the aspect of our mind that relates to concepts, ideas, thoughts and opinions. The yi takes in experiences and organizes them. The yi makes sense of life experiences, which include feelings and emotions. It is involved in forming the ego. The maturity of the yi contributes to how experiences and emotions are processed. For example, if a person is prejudiced toward a race or ethnic group, this prejudice is part of their thinking and concepts in relation to the group. The person processes this prejudice into the earth yi, which then influences the other shen. How we see (hun), hear (zhi), smell (po) and speak (shen) are all influenced by the yi's condition.

A fundamental aspect of the Spleen's function is to hold blood in the blood vessels and assist in circulating blood. On a psychological and emotional level, the yi holds thoughts, opinions and emotions inside the body and distributes them throughout the body. If our yi is clear and balanced, and is mindful of the innate natural virtues of the five shen, those feelings and virtues are circulated throughout the body. The favorable qualities of the Spleen/yi are openness, fairness and receptiveness, including being open to new experiences and the spontaneity of life. The unfavorable qualities include worry, pensiveness, obsessiveness, narrowness, fixation and living in the past—living in past experiences and past conditioned responses to life.

The Spleen and Stomach healing sound is "hoooo" (pronounced like "go"). Begin at the starting position (see Figure 4.1), inhale and move your hands to your abdomen. Your hands should be in lightly clenched fists. Your back should be straight and your body relaxed. Open your eyes and slowly inhale, and in a circular movement bring your hands out to the sides of your body, and then gently up to the Spleen and Stomach area. Place your fingers on your abdomen. Time your inhale to be complete as your hands touch your abdomen. As you exhale, gently move your body a little forward and tuck in your middle abdomen very gently. Make the "*hoooo*" sound as you exhale. You can just make the sound. You can also name and exhale the unfavorable emotions, if they exist. After exhaling, gently move back to the beginning position. Place your hands over your abdomen or on your thighs, smile into the abdomen and breathe softly and gently (see Figure 4.6). Keep your intention (focus) in the Stomach, Spleen and the abdomen. Exhaling is the releasing stage. It releases heat, gas and the unfavorable emotionally charged Qi. The rest stage is the reinforcing stage; it tonifies (supplements) the Spleen and allows the natural virtue of the organ/yi to unfold.

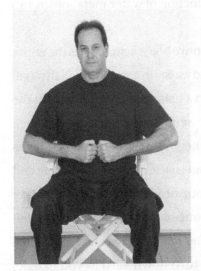

FIGURE 4.6 THE SPLEEN AND STOMACH HEALING SOUND

The San Jiao Healing Sound

The San Jiao is the last of the six healing sounds. The San Jiao is not an organ; it can be translated as the "triple warmer" or "triple burner." The three Jiao comprise the lower, middle and the upper areas of the body. The San Jiao ranges from the feet to the head. From a Qi gong viewpoint, it includes the functioning of the entire body and the circulation of Qi throughout the body. One of its major functions is to maintain a balanced temperature in the body. In Qi gong, it is important to bring heat in the upper areas of the body down to the cooler, lower areas of the body, and the coolness of the lower body to the heat in the upper body. When Qi is circulating within the body, the heat and the coolness mix to create balanced warmth, promoting health and vitality. In Chinese medicine, the San Jiao is involved in two other major functions of the body. The first function is to distribute source Qi throughout the entire body. The San Jiao also assists in the proper function of water metabolism and fluids throughout the body.

The San Jiao influences the entire body; actually, it is the entire body. The San Jiao healing sound assists in circulating Qi through all three Jiao and helps to keep a balanced temperature in the body; these two functions are essential for health and vitality.

The San Jiao healing sound begins in the sitting position. As you inhale, raise your hands out to the sides of your body and extend them fully up above your head, with the palms facing upward. After a full inhale, your hands should be extended above your head. As you exhale, make the "heeee" sound (like "tree"). The hands and palms turn downward as you exhale, moving down the front of your body, from above your head and as far as you can down toward your feet. Time your exhale and your arm movement to be completed simultaneously, as your palms move toward the ground. After exhaling, keep your hands at your knees and breathe naturally (see Figure 4.7). Practice the San Jiao healing sound three times or more. The San Jiao healing sound can be practiced lying down.

FIGURE 4.7 THE SAN JIAO HEALING SOUND

Summary

The healing sounds are a safe, natural way to release unfavorable emotions (emotionally charged Qi), release heat and cool the body. They also tonify the internal organs, allow the natural virtues to be expressed and strengthen the conditions of the internal organs and the health of the body. In the Chinese and Taoist model of the three treasures—Jing (physical), Qi (energy) and Shen (spirit)—an individual can be focused more on just one of these aspects of life. If one is stuck in Jing or the physical aspect of life, the physical becomes a predominant focus. The healing sounds can help one to realize that they are not fundamentally just their physical body and their emotions. The healing sounds begin a process of becoming more aware of the Qi and Shen aspects of life. As these two aspects of life become the focus of the yi (mindfulness), a balance is achieved among the three treasures. This balance is the foundation of health, happiness and vitality.

Medical Qi gong provides an opportunity for people to practice a self-healing method daily in the comfort of their living spaces. The healing sounds can be practiced alone or along with acupuncture and herbal treatments. The combination creates a powerful healing synergy. The healing sounds are a gift from the insights of the early Chinese healers.

Inner-Smile Nei Dan

The inner-smile is the second nei dan practice and it is an extension of the healing sounds. This meditation generates a smiling, loving and relaxing energy and moves it through the internal organs in the controlling (ko) cycle of the five phases. I prefer to call it the "shaping" cycle. Each new organ is shaped by the natural virtues of its preceding organ/shen. The healing sounds flows in the creation (sheng) and the inner-smile flows in the shaping cycle; both cycles create a balanced state of well-being.

The inner-smile can be practiced alone, but it is usually practiced before any of the nei dan practices. The inner-smile is the second part of the healing sounds in the shaping order.

How to practice the inner-smile nei dan:

- Begin by sitting on a chair or on the floor. Your spine should be straight and relaxed, not rigid. Place the tip of your tongue at your palate (the roof of the mouth).

- Hold your hands in your lap in any way that is comfortable for you.

- Begin by smiling for a few minutes. When you feel relaxed, continue to smile and place your mind's attention at the top of your head. Continue to smile throughout the entire meditation.

- Smile as you move your attention down the front and back of your head, and continue down to your neck. There will be two lines we smile down from here: the front and back of the body.

- Continue smiling down your neck to your chest, and then down to the abdomen and then the groin, and continue smiling down your legs to your toes. Continue to smile throughout the meditation.

- Gently move your attention to your shoulders and smile down your back to the lumbar area.

- Gently move your attention back to your shoulders and smile down your arms to your fingers.

- Take as much time as you need until you feel relaxed with the smiling energy.

- Gently bring your attention to the Heart center (between your nipples, behind the sternum). Smile into the Heart center and repeat the words "smiling, loving energy." Continue at the Heart center until you feel smiling energy. This part of the meditation may last a few minutes.

- When you feel the smiling, loving energy at the Heart center, move your attention to your Heart. Repeat the words "joy" and "love." Feel joy and love in your Heart. Do this for 1–5 minutes, or until you feel joy and love. You can also see a red color or cloud in and around the Heart as you smile into it.

- When you feel joy and love in your Heart, move your attention to your Lungs. Smile and repeat the word "courage." Feel courage in your Lungs. Do this until you feel energy in your Lungs. You can also see a white color or cloud in and around the Lungs as you smile into it.

- When you feel energy in your Lungs, move your attention to your Liver. Smile and repeat the word "kindness." Feel kindness in your Liver. Do this until you feel energy in your Liver. You can also see a green color or cloud in and around the Liver as you smile into it.

- When you feel energy in your Liver, move your attention to your Spleen. Smile and repeat the word "openness." Feel openness in your Spleen. Do this until you feel energy in your Spleen. You can also see a yellow or golden color or cloud in and around the Spleen as you smile into it.

- When you feel energy in your Spleen, move your attention to your Kidneys. Smile and repeat the word "gentleness." Feel gentleness in your Kidneys. Do this until you feel energy in your Kidneys. You can also see

a blue-green color or cloud in and around the Kidneys
as you smile into it.

Finish this meditation by gently moving your attention to the
center of the lower dan tian (behind and below the navel).
Focus there for 3–5 minutes. After completing the meditation,
open your eyes, stretch and enjoy. If you are going to continue
with more nei dan practice, gently move on to the small heavenly orbit (microcosmic orbit).

CHAPTER 6

The Eight Extraordinary Channels Nei Dan, Part 1

The Small Heavenly Orbit Nei Dan

The Eight Extraordinary Channels are part of the acupuncture channel system—sinew, luo, main, divergent and the Eight Extraordinary Channels. The Eight Extraordinary Channels are presented in the classic medical texts: the *Nei Jing Su Wen* and *Nei Jing Ling Shu*. There is surprisingly little information on these channels in those two classic books and other early classics. For detailed information on the Eight Extraordinary Channels, see my book *Eight Extraordinary Channels*, published by Singing Dragon. Nei dan practitioners explored the inner body (see the *Nei Jing Tu*, Chapter 9) and traced out the pathways and functions of the Eight Extraordinary Channels. The Inner Map (*Nei Jing Tu*) is the terrain for nei dan.

The Eight Extraordinary Channels are considered the core channels. Core in this context means they are directly connected to Jing (essence). There is no English equivalent for Jing; DNA would be close to the function of Jing. The Eight Extraordinary Channels derive from Jing. In Chinese medicine, the body's Yang cooks the body's Yin, creating a steam or Qi. That Qi is the first Qi, which is called yuan Qi (original Qi). Yuan Qi is Jing in Qi form. I follow the view that the first acupuncture channel created is the Chong channel. It is Jing in channel form. Because it comes from Jing, it contains the DNA code of each person. The Chong channel flows throughout the body with its Jing code to create the remaining Eight Extraordinary Channels and then all the channels of the body. The condition of the Chong channel has a direct influence on all channels and the entire body. The Chong, Ren and Du channels all originate in the Lower Jiao—that means in the Jing. All three are considered the core channels and have a significant influence on the other channels and the entire body.

When the Eight Extraordinary Channels are open and flowing in a normal way, the body's vital substances circulate normally, creating health and vitality. Unfavorable conditioning can influence the Eight Extraordinary Channels and physical and psycho-emotional health. Obtaining and maintaining healthy Eight Extraordinary Channels is an essential aspect of the nei dan presented in this book.

The first nei dan practice that includes the Eight Extraordinary Channels is the small heavenly orbit (microcosmic orbit). The orbit is comprised of the Ren and Du channels, the main channels that flow up the back of the body and down the front of the body (Figure 6.2).

The Small Heavenly Orbit (the Microcosmic Orbit)

The small heavenly orbit is comprised of the Ren and Du channels, which are the acupuncture channels that flow up the back of the body, and then down the front of the body (Figure 6.2). This circuit has a few names, such as the heavenly orbit, small heavenly orbit, the orbit and the microcosmic orbit. The Chinese name is *Xiao Zhou Tian*; it is the foundational nei dan inner meditation. Lifestyle, poor diet, poor posture and emotional imbalances can cause blockages in this circular orbit. By practicing nei dan, we can clear, cleanse and energize these core channels. The efficiency of the functioning of the Ren–Du orbit has a direct influence on the entire the body.

Lower Dan Tian

Life begins in the lower dan tian (Figure 6.1). Therefore, we begin nei dan practices in the lower dan tian. This dan tian is located in the lower center of the body below the navel; it is the body's energetic root and foundation. The lower dan tian is often called the sea of Qi. It is the origin of the source Qi and the origin of Kidney Yin and Kidney Yang. These vital substances ignite, fuel and vitalize the entire body. Physically, the uterus is the location of creation and it is located in the lower dan tian.

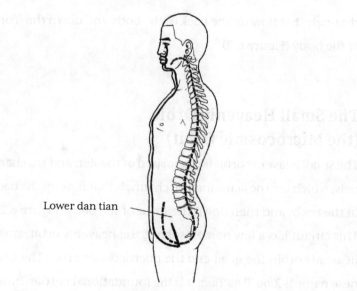

Lower dan tian

FIGURE 6.1 LOWER DAN TIAN

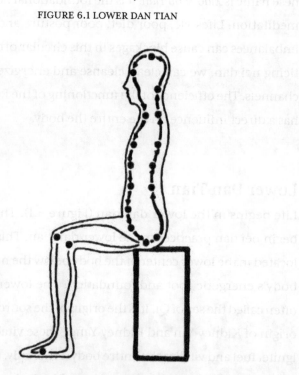

FIGURE 6.2 THE SMALL HEAVENLY ORBIT

We begin our practice by focusing our attention in the sea of Qi. In nei dan and Qi gong theory, "focusing attention" is under the control of the Spleen and the yi. Wherever we focus our attention, Qi moves to that area. When focusing into the lower dan tian, Qi will be directed there. As Qi fills the lower dan tian, it energizes the area, including the organs, the glands and all the functions of the area. This begins the process of rejuvenation. When the lower dan tian is rejuvenated, the entire body benefits.

Location

The location of where to focus our attention in the lower dan tian can vary. It is commonly described as behind the umbilicus and one to three inches below it. This is the approximate area. My suggestion is to place your attention in this area and move your attention around until you feel something locally. It can be a feeling of fullness, tingling, denseness, energy or a pull. The location can change from day to day. Feeling guides the location. Indeed, feeling will be the guiding principle behind the entire practice. If you do not feel anything, continue with one of the methods presented in this chapter, and with time and practice you will begin to feel the Qi.

As the lower dan tian fills with Qi, it is restored to a level of homeostasis. As this area fills up, Qi will move throughout the body according to a built-in intelligence and channel system. Nei dan is a way to enhance the flow of Qi through the body. It will clear blockages, reduce excesses, supplement deficiencies and rejuvenate the body.

Beginning Nei Dan

Nei dan begins with being centered and relaxed. A way to allow this feeling to occur is by focusing attention in the lower dan tian. There are a few ways to practice focusing. Two of them are now described.

Method 1: Focusing

Begin by focusing on a fixed point or area within the lower dan tian. This is *fixed breathing*. Keep your attention on the area as you breathe naturally. During fixed breathing, inhaling draws Qi to the area and exhaling retains the Qi. This process of keeping attention on an area gathers and retains Qi to the area, filling it up with Qi. As the sea of Qi is filled with Qi, the Qi then naturally flows throughout the body. Practice this cultivation for 1–20 minutes or more; do not overdo it. I would not do it for more than 30 minutes for the first year. There is no hurry. Build up the length of your practice in a comfortable way.

Method 2: Spinning

A second method is based on *spinning*. The Taoists were cosmologists; they observed the stars and planets, and they noticed that they flowed in predictable patterns. Often, we do not even notice the most obvious activities around us. Earth is a planet floating in space; it is constantly spinning, in perpetual movement. Guided by the flow of the stars and planets, the ancients turned their attention inward and could feel Qi moving in their body. They practiced methods to enhance internal spinning and circulation. Spinning causes Qi to move to an area. Spinning gathers, collects and accumulates Qi. Spinning is a way to create the movement of Qi; focusing is a way to guide the Qi. Combining both of these methods is a way to gather and guide Qi. Begin by focusing attention in the lower dan tian. Then, after a minute or two, begin spinning. This is done by visualizing a point that is spinning within a small space—the size of a marble or a pearl. You can spin clockwise or counter-clockwise. You can mix the directions up; move in one direction and then the other direction. Keep spinning until you feel the Qi responding to it. Spinning is commonly done three, six, nine, 12, 18, 27 or 36 times. Do this in both directions, and do it until you feel Qi. Be consistent in your spinning. If you spin nine times in one direction, then spin nine times in the other direction. Feeling Qi is most important, not the number of times one spins.

Perform this focus/spin practice until you feel Qi. Select one method or combine the two: you can do only the focus method, only the spinning method or a combination of both methods. Practice this part of nei dan until you feel Qi in the lower dan tian, which can take from a week to a few months. Feeling the Qi is more important than just using any particular numerical pattern (spinning in patterns of three, six, nine or more).

The Small Heavenly Orbit

The small heavenly orbit is the circuit consisting of the Du and Ren channels (Figure 6.2). In this nei dan practice, guide your focus from the center of the lower dan tian down to the Hui Yin point (Ren 1, the perineum), which is about an inch above the anus. From Hui Yin, guide your attention/yi up to the crown, to the Bai Hui point (Du 20, the crown center at the head vertex). This process guides attention up the Du channel. The next step is to guide your focus down the front of the body and back to the Hui Yin point at the perineum. In so doing, your attention has been guided down the Ren channel. Having returned to Hui Yin, you have completed one circuit through the small heavenly orbit.

There are various ways to practice this nei dan. Three methods are presented below.

The First Small Heavenly Orbit Method

The first way is to connect the circulation up the Du channel and down the Ren channel with your breath.

- Throughout this nei dan, your breathing should be natural, relaxed and gentle. Breathe from your lower dan tian.

- Begin by connecting to the center/the lower dan tian. Focus and/or spin in the center until you feel Qi.

- Inhale gently into the center. Stay relaxed and do not change the rate of your breathing. Exhale and gently move your attention to the Hui Yin area at the perineum.

- From the Hui Yin area, inhale up the Du channel (in front of the spine) as you count "one." Gently guide your mind up the Du channel to the crown (the Bai Hui point). Review the picture of the orbit (Figure 6.2) to visualize the area up the back channel.

- The inhale should be completed when you arrive at the crown, at the top of the head.

- Next, guide your focus/attention down the Ren channel. Thus, during the exhale guide your attention from the crown to Hui Yin. Think the number "two," as you flow down the front channel.

- Yang numbers are odd and correspond to ascent. Count an odd number as you inhale up the back (the Du channel). Yin numbers are even and correspond to descent. Count an even number as you exhale down the front of the body (the Ren channel).

- Continue this circulation up the back and down the front for ten cycles. This completes one round.

- Repeat this practice for three, six or nine rounds. Do it until you feel the Qi flowing in the small heavenly orbit.

A goal of the nei dan is to increase the flow of Qi in the channels. Attention or focus guides Qi. Moving your attention up the Du and down the Ren increases Qi flow in the channels and assists in breaking through any stagnations or blockages. This process both increases energy and refines your Qi. Consistent practice strengthens the internal organs, the glands and the brain.

This orbit also influences all the energetic channels in the body. In other words, it benefits the entire body. The Qi, the channels and the body are one inseparable whole.

Gathering Qi

Gathering Qi at the end of each nei dan practice is essential for building and storing Qi and rejuvenating the body. There are various methods of gathering and storing, two of which are described here. Select the method that you feel is more effective. You can alternate or mix the methods.

First, when finishing the practice, gently bring your attention to the center of the lower dan tian. In the center, repeat the method used at the beginning of the practice. With your attention, spin in clockwise and counter-clockwise directions; spin in cycles of nine or 18 in each direction, until you feel the Qi gathering. The range of your spinning can be the size of a marble or a pearl. If over time you feel the need to expand the size, you can do so. When you finish spinning, gently stop and keep your attention fixed in the center in the lower dan tian.

An alternative method to finish the practice is to bring your attention to the center of the lower dan tian and then keep your attention fixed as you inhale and exhale (fixed breathing). With your mind fixed in the center, each inhale draws Qi there and each exhale stores Qi there. As you fill the center with Qi, you are building the root Qi of the entire body. This Qi will flow into all the channels and organs to rejuvenate the body.

The Second Small Heavenly Orbit Method

In this method, guide your attention/yi up the Du and down the Ren channels without connecting the circulation to your breath or counting. Circulate through the orbit at a comfortable pace. Continue the circulation through the orbit until you feel Qi. Complete this meditation by gathering and collecting Qi in the center of the lower dan tian.

The Third Small Heavenly Orbit Method

In this method, bring your attention to major points/centers along the heavenly orbit (listed below). Begin by circulating through the orbit, next work on one or two points, and then continue circulating through the orbit. Start by focusing your attention below and behind the navel. Spin clockwise and counter-clockwise either based on numbers (for example, multiples of nine) or until you feel Qi. Stay balanced in the amount of clockwise and counter-clockwise spinning. When you feel Qi, gently move to the next point on the orbit and repeat the process. Continue this process for as many of the major points on the orbit as you wish to work on. There is no rigid rule as to how many points to work on in one sitting so be flexible, but always follow the order of the points listed below. It may take time to open all the points. Always close the meditation in the normal way by gathering and storing Qi in the center of the lower dan tian.

Always begin in the order listed here. You can try one or two points, then circulate through the orbit, and finally close by gathering Qi in the lower dan tian. There is no rigid rule as to how many points to work on in one sitting. Be flexible.

Energy Centers—the Chakras

From a nei dan viewpoint, the vibration from the Du and Ren channels creates energy centers. That is the front–back and Yang–Yin energies vibrating and interacting. The commonly known seven chakras are similar, but the heavenly orbit has more than seven pairs of paired Yin–Yang points; it has more than seven centers.

Begin by finding the center (near the navel) in the lower tian and move from point to point along the small heavenly orbit. The range is from the navel to a few inches below and inside the body.

- Shen Que, Ren 8

- Qi Hai, Ren 6

- Guan Yuan, Ren 4

- Zhong Ji, Ren 3

- Hui Yin, Ren 1, perineum

- Coccyx, Chang Qiang, Du 1

- Lumbar 2, Ming Men, Du 4

- Thoracic vertebra 11, Ji Zhong, spinal center, adrenal center, Du 6

- Thoracic vertebra 5, Shen Dao, Spirit Path, Du 11, opposite the Heart

- Cervical vertebra 7, Da Zhui, big vertebra, Du 14, opposite the throat

- Cervical vertebra 1, Ya Men, Gate of Muteness, Du 15

- Crown, Bai Hui, Hundred Meetings, Du 20

- Third eye, Yin Tang, mid-eyebrow

- Palate, Hsuan Ying, Heavenly Pool

- Throat, Tian Tu, Heaven's Chimney, Ren 22

- The location is at the fourth intercostal space behind the sternum

- Tan Zhong, Ren 17

- Solar plexus, Zhong Wan, middle of the Stomach, Ren 12

- Umbilicus, Shen Que, Ren 8

After opening the point(s), circulate Qi through the orbit, and then close by gathering Qi in the center of the lower dan tian. Smile throughout the meditation.

Some nei dan traditions have females circulate up the Ren channel (water path, Yin path) and down the Du channel (fire path, Yang path). This is circulating up the front channel and down the back channel in the small heavenly orbit. I use both methods. I may start up the back and down the front, and then practice up the front and down the back channel. I finish by circulating up the back channel and down the front channel. Continue circulating in the directional flow until you feel Qi. Circulating both ways can assist in balancing the Yin and Yang energies in the body. Follow how you feel. Always be guided by your feeling. I suggest you always finish the orbit with the fire path: up the back channel and down the front channel. Complete the meditation by gathering Qi in the center of the lower dan tian.

The Yin–Yang of Nei Dan Inner Meditation

The orbit meditation is the foundation practice of nei dan. It has two main parts. The first part includes Yang practices—internal movements of Qi. For example, guiding Qi through the orbit. The second part is a Yin practice—a stillness practice. The nei dan practitioner combines Yin and Yang practices.

Yang nei dan practice is a shaping process. Directing Qi through the organs and channels is strategically shaping the way Qi flows in the body based on a deep understanding of the acupuncture channel system. These practices stimulate the innate intelligence of the body, mind and spirit. A goal of the Yang practice is to restore the normal functions of the three treasures. The Yin practice is an "allowing" process. By sitting in stillness, we allow the fruits of the Yang nei dan to manifest. In this part of nei dan, we let go and just be—be aware of our aliveness (spiritual awareness), no more and no less. If the mind wanders, just gently focus back on the awareness. Wandering is normal. Nei dan practice resets our awareness from the stresses of life. The quick reset to our normal, natural, spiritual awareness is a fruit of nei dan cultivation.

Yin Nei Dan

Nei dan is like cooking. The cook prepares the ingredients and then cooks them. Timing is crucial to the cooking; time that allows the food to sit is crucial, too. Sitting allows time to capture the benefits of the cooking. We include just sitting in our nei dan. Upon completion of the Yang nei dan practice, we then practice Yin nei dan—stillness nei dan. This will become the most enjoyable part of the nei dan. We work to increase the duration of the Yin nei dan in our daily practice. There will be times when you spend more time in the Yin nei dan aspect of the practice; that is normal and a goal of nei dan. As you experience the benefits of nei dan, the amount of time needed to attune to your spirit decreases. The Yin nei dan awareness is your natural self; with practice, this becomes our everyday consciousness.

Before Thinking

In Zen Buddhism, there is a state of awareness that occurs when one shifts their attention to "before thinking." In my experience, Yin nei dan is before thinking; nei dan leads a person to before thinking, which is *awareness of aliveness*. These are different traditions pointing to the same awareness; it is the shared reality among all people. We all have the free will and freedom to attune to this awareness.

Yin or Yang Nei Dan?

Be flexible as you learn nei dan. As you practice and get used to the nei dan practice, move back and forth from Yang to Yin nei dan as you feel necessary. Work toward spending more time in Yin nei dan.

Nei Dan vs. Meditation

Nei dan includes meditation. It also includes a deep understanding of the human body from a Chinese medical viewpoint, including the acupuncture system. One part of nei dan is designed to assist in restoring the body to health, vitality and longevity. This is what distinguishes nei dan from other meditation methods, which do not have the same emphasis on the healing aspects. Nei dan includes medical Qi gong and spiritual practice; we enjoy the fruit of both.

CHAPTER 7

The Eight Extraordinary Channels Nei Dan, Part 2

The Eight Extraordinary Channels nei dan inner meditation includes guiding Qi through those channels and areas of the body. The Eight Extraordinary Channels are big channels; they are like seas, not streams. They cover large areas of the body. The acupuncture channel pictures presented in this chapter and in acupuncture books show thin lines for the channels, giving the impression that the channels are thin, but they are actually big pathways of Qi flow. In our nei dan practice, we move our attention into these big channels to increase the circulation of Qi (bioelectricity) to clear and energize the channels and the surrounding areas they influence.

The Wei and Qiao Channels Nei Dan

The Wei channels were added to the acupuncture channel system after the earliest acupuncture book in the Han dynasty—the *Ling Shu*. The Wei and Qiao channels are very close together, so for this nei dan practice we combine them into one.

Yang Wei and Yang Qiao Practice 1: From Feet to Hips

This cultivation begins with the lateral aspects of the legs: the Yang Wei and Yang Qiao channels (see Figures 7.1a and b). This meditation starts in the center of the lower dan tian, the origin of life and the extraordinary channels. From the center, our attention is then guided through the heavenly orbit: the Du and Ren channels. After these core channels are open and you feel the Qi flowing, move your focus to the leg channels: the Yang Wei and Yang Qiao channels. Notice the locations of the beginning of the two channels in Figures 7.1a and b; they originate at the lateral aspect of the foot, underneath the lateral ankle.

Move your attention from the center of the lower dan tian over to the hips, and then down the lateral aspect of the legs to below the lateral ankle. Place your attention at the external part of the foot. As you inhale, move your mind up to the hips. Then exhale back down the lateral part of the legs to the feet. Trace the areas shown in Figures 7.1a and b. Repeat this process nine or 18 times until you feel the Qi. Doing that clears and energizes the leg channels.

This meditation can be practiced on one side followed by the other, or it can be practiced on both sides at the same time.

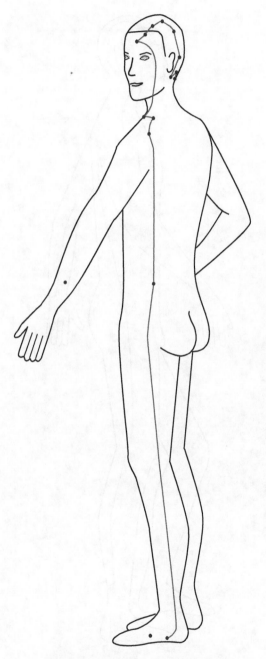

FIGURE 7.1A THE YANG WEI CHANNEL

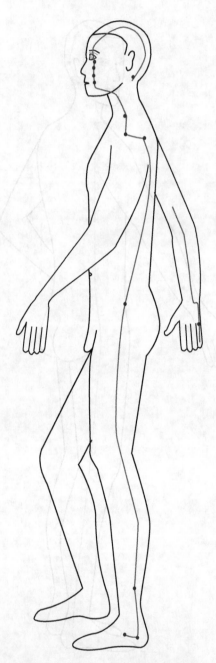

FIGURE 7.1B THE YANG QIAO CHANNEL

Yin Wei and Yin Qiao Practice 1:
From Feet to Hips

Once Qi is felt in the Yang Wei and Yang Qiao channels, move to the Yin Wei and Yin Qiao channels (Figures 7.2a and b). Repeat the process already practiced on the Yang Wei and Yang Qiao channels. Begin by bringing your attention to below the medial ankle at the bottom of the feet. As you inhale, guide your attention up the inner thighs to the pubic bone. The channels are an inch or two inside the body; with practice, you will actively feel it. Time your inhale so that it finishes as you reach the pubic bone. Exhale as you guide your attention back down the inner legs, to the starting point. Repeat this practice of inhaling up the legs and exhaling down the legs, for a cycle of nine times. Continue practicing in sets of nine or until you feel Qi.

Yang Wei and Yang Qiao Practice 2:
From Feet to Hips and then to Brain

This practice continues from the previous Yang Wei–Yang Qiao practice, expanding beyond the hips and flowing up the channels along the sides of the body to the shoulders, neck, head and brain. The practice begins at the bottom of the feet. As you inhale, guide your attention up and along the sides of the body to the hips, shoulders, neck, front of the face, around the temples, to the occipital area and into the brain. This should be a soft, gentle inhale, connected with the process of guiding your attention and Qi along the channels into the brain. As you exhale, guide your attention back down the channels to the bottom of the feet. One round is one inhale up and one exhale down. One set is nine rounds. Repeat a number of rounds until you feel Qi in these channels.

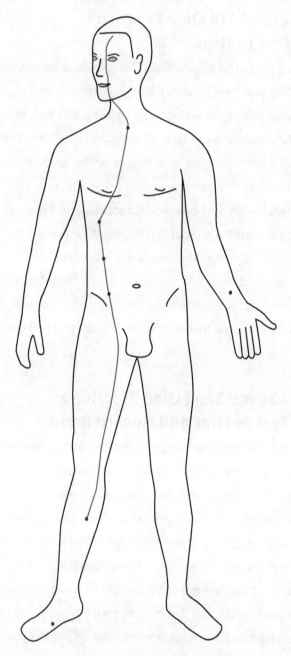

FIGURE 7.2A THE YIN WEI CHANNEL

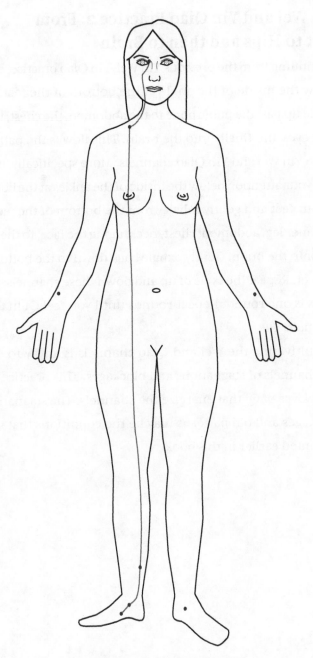

FIGURE 7.2B THE YIN QIAO CHANNEL

Yin Wei and Yin Qiao Practice 2: From Feet to Hips and then to Brain

Continuing from the previous Yin Wei–Yin Qiao practice, begin below the inside of the ankle at the bottom of the feet, and inhale up past the pubic bone to the abdomen, the chest, neck, face, eyes and finally into the brain. This flow is the pathway of the Yin Wei and Yin Qiao channels. More specifically, begin with your attention below the inside of the ankles at the bottom of your feet and gently inhale from the bottom of the feet up the inner leg, abdomen, chest, neck, along the face, to the eyes and into the brain. Gently exhale back down to the bottom of the feet. Repeat the cycle of up and down these channels: nine times is one round. Repeat rounds until you feel Qi in these channels.

Cultivating the Wei and Qiao channels is a way to clear the channels of stagnations and blockages. This practice creates waves of Qi that energize the channels. The stagnations, blockages and old patterns may be the conditions that were presented earlier in this book.

The Dai Channel Nei Dan

The Dai channel, or Dai Mai, is the belt channel. It is a unique channel because it is the only horizontal channel of the Eight Extraordinary Channels. It connects the right and left sides of the body, as well as the upper and lower areas of the body; it unifies all the channels and areas of the body. From a nei dan perspective, it has four major functions: it connects the left and right sides, the upper and lower, and the interior and exterior areas of the body, and it is also a protective shield from the exterior. It is a wei Qi (protective Qi) field.

The Dai channel also plays an important role in filtering. This filtering process includes all the Eight Extraordinary Channels, as well as the interior and exterior of the body. As a belt holds things in, this channel can hold things. The things it can hold include emotions, trauma and pathogenic factors. When the belt channel is not functioning properly, pathogens are held which can create more imbalances and stresses on the body. It is essential to clear the belt channel to allow proper filtering in the body. The belt channel is also a protective Qi field that guards against exterior factors such as wind, cold and heat. It also protects against influences from other people. Clearing the belt channel helps maintain the effective filtering of pathogens and life experiences. It helps to keep what is beneficial and to let go of what is not healthy. All the nei dan practices contribute to building your energy, and that energy fills the Dai Mai, allowing it to effectively function.

In acupuncture theory, the Dai channel has a narrow pathway. In Qi gong and nei dan, it is a pathway that covers the entire body, similar to the San Jiao channel (Figure 7.3).

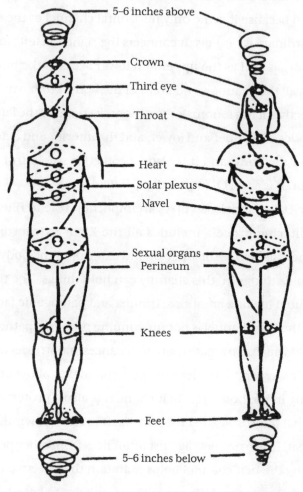

5–6 inches above

Crown

Third eye

Throat

Heart

Solar plexus

Navel

Sexual organs
Perineum

Knees

Feet

5–6 inches below

Clockwise turning   Counter-clockwise turning

FIGURE 7.3 THE NEI DAN DAI CHANNEL

Dai Channel Nei Dan, Part 1

The Dai channel nei dan begins in the lower dan tian. This meditation connects the front, right, back and left aspects of the body. It also connects the Ren and Du channels.

After practicing the microcosmic orbit and the Wei/Qiao channel meditations, begin by focusing your attention on the center of the lower dan tian. After you feel Qi, move your attention in a clockwise circle inside the body at the level of the umbilicus/Shen Que, Ren 8. Spin the Qi an inch or two inside the body nine, 18 or more times clockwise and then the same number of times counter-clockwise, until you feel Qi. You may feel the Qi with fewer spirals than 18, in which case, you can stop and continue to the next part of the practice. With practice, the Qi feeling will begin to arrive faster. This spinning process continues at nine different levels in the body, as well as below the feet and above the head. Spin clockwise as you ascend and counter-clockwise as you descend these levels. The order of the levels is as follows:

1. Navel center, Shen Que, Ren 8

2. Solar plexus center, Zhong Wan, Ren 12

3. Heart center, Tan Zhong, Ren 17

4. Throat center, Ren Ying, Stomach 9

5. Third eye center, Yin Tang

6. Crown center, Bai Hui, Du 20

7. Move your focus to a point a few inches above your head, and spin for a few seconds, then descend counter-clockwise in long spirals, from Du 20 to the perineum

8. Perineum, Hui Yin, Ren 1

9. Knee center, Wei Zhong, Bladder 40

10. Ankle center, Tai Xi, Kidney 3 and Shen Mai, Bladder 62

11. Move your focus to a point a few inches below your feet and spiral for a few seconds. Then spiral from below the feet in a clockwise pattern from below the feet to above the head. Repeat this descending and ascending spiraling three, six or nine times, until you feel the Qi. Do a clockwise pattern when ascending and a counter-clockwise pattern when descending.

To finish this nei dan, gently guide your attention to the center of the lower dan tian, and then continue to move in the microcosmic orbit until you feel Qi. Finally, complete this cultivation by collecting Qi at the center in the lower dan tian.

Dai Channel Nei Dan, Part 2

When you feel Qi in each of the energy centers in the Dai channel, move to the center of the lower dan tian. Then move upward in long spirals, moving up to the crown and above the head in a clockwise flow. Then reverse the flow, moving counter-clockwise and downward to below the feet. In this process, make long spirals, ascending up the channel and then descending down the channel. Repeat this pattern until you feel the Qi. Close this meditation by gently moving your attention to the center of the lower dan tian and gather Qi.

The Chong Channel Nei Dan

The Chong channel is also called the "thrusting channel." This channel is the *core* channel. It is the closest channel to the center of the body and its Jing. The Chong channel is considered the central processing unit of the body. Clearing and energizing this channel has a profound influence on all the channels and the three treasures of life. The Chong channel nei dan completes the Eight Extraordinary Channels part of this nei dan.

The Chong channel can be viewed in two ways. The first is as one channel. The second way is to view the Chong channel in three sections: the first section is the center, the second section is the right side, and the third is the left side—all three are actually one (Figure 7.4). The nei dan process of circulating Qi in the Chong channel is the same as described for the other channels.

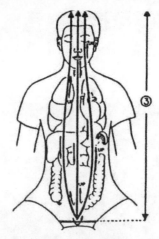

FIGURE 7.4 THE NEI DAN CHONG CHANNEL

Chong Channel Nei Dan Practice 1

The first nei dan method is based on viewing the Chong channel as one channel. Begin by moving your attention to the perineum. As you inhale, guide your attention up to the crown. As you exhale, guide your attention back down to the perineum. Repeat this method of inhaling up and exhaling down, which comprises one round. Repeat this for up to nine rounds or until you feel Qi. Inhaling upward and exhaling downward should be done gently, keeping the body relaxed at all times. Feeling Qi is a goal of this practice. When you feel Qi, do this practice a few more rounds until the Qi builds. Then, to finish this nei dan, bring your attention back to the center in the lower dan tian and collect the Qi there.

Collecting Qi in the center of the lower dan tian concludes every practice. Your breathing should be done in a relaxed and gentle way. Do not create any stress or rigidity in the body during this practice.

Chong Channel Nei Dan Practice 2

The second method for the Chong channel nei dan is to view the channel in three sections. The first area is the center of the perineum; it flows up the center of the body to the center of the brain. The second area is the right side of the perineum; it flows up the right side of the body to the right side of the brain. The third area is the left side of the perineum; it flows up the left side of the body to the left side of the brain.

Begin this practice in the center of the perineum. Repeat the same method for each section of the Chong channel. Begin by guiding your attention to the center of the perineum. As you inhale, guide your attention up the center of the body to the center of the brain. As you exhale, guide your attention down the body to the center of the perineum. Then gently move your attention to the right side and repeat the inhalation and exhalation, up and down the right side of the channel. Repeat this process in the center of the perineum, then to the left side of the channel. Then move to the center of the perineum. Repeat this process from the center, right, center, left and the center to complete one round. Practice this sequence up to nine rounds or until you feel the Qi.

To finish this part of the nei dan, gently guide your attention to the center of the lower dan tian. Then move into the microcosmic orbit until you feel Qi in this orbit pathway. Complete this cultivation by collecting Qi in the center of the lower dan tian.

Practice the entire Eight Extraordinary Channels nei dan until you feel Qi in each of the channels. Follow the exact order given in this chapter until you feel Qi flowing in all the channels. When you feel Qi in all the channels, change the order of practice to the following sequence, which will be the way to practice from now on:

1. Begin in the center in the lower dan tian.

2. Du channel.

3. Ren channel.

4. Continue in the small heavenly orbit until Qi is felt.

5. Chong channel.

6. Dai channel.

7. Yin Qiao–Yin Wei channels.

8. Yang Qiao–Yang Wei channels.

9. Circulate Qi in the small heavenly orbit.

10. Close by gathering Qi in the center of the lower dan tian.

This completes the Eight Extraordinary Channels nei dan. Practice this nei dan for six months to a year before moving to the next nei dan practice—five shen nei dan.

CHAPTER 8

Five Shen Nei Dan Inner Meditation

The five shen nei dan inner meditation is a beautiful example of applying five-phases correspondences in a valuable practice that can have a wonderful influence on your life. This nei dan cultivation (meditation) further develops the process of turning the focus/intention inward that was described in the previous nei dan practices. This focusing of the attention is a function of the yi. We use the yi to develop our conscious intention and ability to turn inward, and thus move our life force inward and throughout the body. This ability to focus the intentional direction is an essential aspect of this practice.

Balance is the key to health, vitality and longevity. The five shen cultivation balances the energies of the body. This practice transforms life force (Qi, bioelectricity) from imbalance to balance. Table 8.1 lists the five-phases correspondences used in the five shen cultivation.

The Cauldron

A cauldron is a large pot (kettle) that is used for cooking. Nei dan (alchemy) is a type of cooking. When cooking food, there is a synergy that occurs in the cauldron. The food and fluids are cooked, thereby creating something new. The result is achieved through the integration of the cauldron, food, fluids and heat. Similar to this physical cauldron, we have an energetic cauldron in the nei dan inner meditation. The energies of the organs and their correspondences are mixed and transformed in this cauldron, which is located in the solar plexus area; this area is the middle center (Middle Jiao) in this nei dan practice. The energies of the organs are brought into this cauldron to be mixed, integrated and transformed. This is the *fusion of the five phases* (five correspondences). These energies are transformed to original Qi (yuan Qi), which is the life force that can rejuvenate the body.

In Chinese medicine, the first energy in the body is called original Qi. This Qi will transform into the Qi of the organs, glands, bones, tendons, blood, brain and the entire body. It is the life force that is derived from Jing/essence, and it is the basis of the body, mind and spirit. Each of the organs has its own Qi—for example, Kidney Qi, Liver Qi, Heart Qi, Spleen Qi and Lung Qi. When the original Qi flows into the organs, the nature of the original Qi changes to the nature of the organs. The original Qi is the most neutral Qi; it is similar to a stem cell, since it can take the shape, form and quality of the different parts of the body. Say, for example, we try to relive a past experience or perhaps we have some experience that is very impactful on our life; in that situation, part of our life force (Qi) transforms into that experience or emotion. Consequently, we always have the capacity to change our life force, whether favorably or unfavorably. In nei dan, we seek to change or transform our life force to its original Qi state. This allows the natural virtues of the organs to materialize. It allows us to be a living expression of our spirit.

The cauldron for the nei dan of emotional work is located in the middle of the body. This middle center is also called the Middle Jiao. In general, the lower center is behind and below the navel; the middle center is behind the solar plexus; and the upper center is behind the Heart center. The lower center corresponds to the Kidneys; the middle center corresponds to the Spleen and Stomach; and the upper center corresponds to the Lungs and the Heart. The Spleen is the earth phase, which is the transformation phase. The earth phase can transform the other phases into their natural Qi. In nei dan, we seek to transform imbalanced Qi into balanced Qi, and then subsequently into original Qi. This original Qi is then guided into the organs and the acupuncture channels (the terrain for Qi flow), where it is moved throughout the entire body. As a result of this energetic circulation, the body can be healed and rejuvenated. Fusion of the five phases is a profound inner cultivation that transforms emotions and five-phase imbalances into vitality. This cultivation assists in harmonizing the emotional body, allowing awareness of the spirit body.

Preparation

Begin with the inner-smile meditation and then practice the small heavenly orbit for a few minutes until you feel the Qi flowing in the body. When you feel the Qi flowing in the small heavenly orbit, you can decide to continue with the Eight Extraordinary Channels nei dan or begin the five shen nei dan.

The Five Shen Nei Dan

Begin by sitting in a chair with your back straight and your chin tucked in gently. This posture allows the Qi to flow smoothly up the back and to the brain—this is the Du channel. It then flows down the front of the body—the Ren channel. Turn your focus inward to the center in the lower dan tian. This is the area behind and below the navel. It is not a fixed point: wherever you feel Qi, or a sensation, is where the center of the lower dan tian is located. Place your attention in the center. Allow this awareness to become stronger. Practice this meditation until you feel the Qi.

Table 8.1 Five-phases correspondences

Shen	Organ	Sensory organ	Sense	Temperature	Emotion	Color/Element
Shen	Heart / Small Intestine	Tongue	Taste	Hot	Hastiness, impatience, hatred, arrogance	Red / Fire
Zhi	Kidneys / Bladder	Ears	Hearing	Cold, wet	Fear, paranoia	Blue, green, black, blue / Water
Hun	Liver / Gallbladder	Eyes	Sight	Warm, moist	Anger, irritability, frustration	Green / Wood
Po	Lungs / Large Intestine	Nose	Smell	Cool, dry	Sadness, depression, loneliness	White / Metal
Yi	Spleen / Stomach	Mouth	Eating	Mild	Worry, pensiveness	Yellow / Earth

Smiling into the Five Organs

The five shen correspondences are presented in Chapters 2 and 4 of this book. Some of these correspondences are applied in this cultivation. Having a clear understanding of the physical locations of the five organs is the first step in the practice. You may need to refer to a good anatomy book. In addition to learning to focus on the actual organs, we set up the energy (qi) collection points for the organs (see Figure 8.1) and visualize these collection points, as they become an essential aspect of this cultivation.

Begin this practice by placing your attention in the Kidneys. When doing this, you are connecting your life force (Qi) and the organ. The Qi and the organ are integrated, and the organ is energized. This is the beginning process of creating vitality and rejuvenation. Don't just place your attention in the Kidneys—*smile* into the Kidneys. Smiling is an essential aspect of the practice; it creates a transformative life force that can change the emotional condition of a person.

- When you feel the Kidneys filled with Qi—a smiling Qi—move to the next organ.

- Gently move your attention into the Heart. Concentrate with a relaxed body and mind, and smile into the Heart. Focus in and around the entire Heart until you feel the Heart filled with Qi. When you feel the Qi in the Heart, gently move to the Liver.

- Focus in and around the Liver until you feel the Liver full of Qi. Smile into the Liver and fill it with smiling energy. When you feel the Liver full of energy, gently move your focus into the Lungs.

- Smile into the Lungs. When you feel the Lungs filled with Qi, gently move your attention into the Spleen.

- Smile into the Spleen and fill it with energy.

After you have focused on the Spleen, become aware of all five organs. Focus your attention on all the organs; feel the energy of each of the five organs. Spend up to ten minutes in this organ-awareness meditation. This meditation begins the *fusion of the five phases* nei dan inner meditation. Finish this nei dan by gently moving your attention and Qi to the lower dan tian and collect the energy there.

Spend up to a few months practicing this meditation. Practice until you feel the smiling energy in all five organs. Being able to feel the Qi in the organs integrates your life force and your organs—the Qi and the body; it is the beginning step in self-awareness and self-realization.

The Five Phases (Five Elements)

This part of the nei dan includes the five elements of nature. The process is similar to the previous cultivation of smiling into the organs. Smiling into an organ connects the organ and its Qi. In this cultivation, we connect an organ and its element.

This fusion of the body (the internal organs) and Qi revital-izes the life force of the organs and the organ itself. Continue from the smiling into the organ part of this nei dan. Begin in the Kidneys: smile into the Kidneys until you feel the Qi of the Kidneys. When you feel the Qi of the Kidneys, visualize and feel the energy of water. Visualize an ocean, river, lake or a body of water you are familiar with. Feel the water. Connect your yi to the water. Bring this water awareness to your Kidneys. Feel the water in your Kidneys. Smile into the Kidneys and feel the water Qi. Continue this nei dan until you feel the water Qi.

When you feel the water Qi, gently move your attention to the Heart. Smile into the Heart. When you feel the smiling Qi in the Heart, feel warm fire energy. A good source of fire energy is the sun. If you prefer, become aware of the nourishing heat and fire of the sun. Allow this warming fire to grow in the Heart. Smile into the fire energy in the Heart.

When you feel the fire energy of the Heart, gently move your attention to the Liver. Smile into the Liver. When you feel the smiling energy in the Liver, visualize trees in the forest or trees in some location you have experienced. Feel the trees, which is the wood element. Fill the Liver with this wood energy. Spend a few minutes or longer until you feel the wood energy.

When you feel the wood energy in the Liver, gently move your attention to the Lungs. Smile into the Lungs until you feel the smiling energy of the Lungs. The Lungs are the metal element. Visualize natural metal in our environment. Allow this feeling of metal to manifest. Smile and guide the metal feeling into the Lungs. Fill the Lungs with metal energy. Allow this energy to grow in the Lungs. Mix the smiling energy and the metal energy in the Lungs. Sit with this metal feeling in the Lungs.

When you feel the metal energy fill the Lungs, gently move your attention to the Spleen. Smile into the Spleen. Visualize earth Qi. It can be a place you have visited or lived. It can be the mountains you have experienced. Feel this mountain energy. Feel the earth energy in the Spleen. Allow this energy to fill the Spleen. Mix the earth energy and the smiling energy. Continue at this stage for a few minutes or until you strongly feel the earth energy.

Practice this nei dan for a few weeks or months, or until you feel the elements in each organ. It is ideal to practice in the natural environments where each element in this nei dan practice can be found. Continue to the next part of this nei dan or finish this nei dan by gently guiding your energy and attention to the center of the lower dan tian and collect the energy.

The Colors of the Organs

The five Yin organs house the five shen. Each of the organs has a color. When the organ and its life force are balanced, the color of the organ is vibrant. In this part of the nei dan, visualize the middle center, the solar plexus area, which is the Spleen and the Stomach, filled with a yellow or golden color. Visualize a vibrant yellow or golden sphere. This is the earth phase, and it is a transformer. The order in which we flow from organ to organ follows the previous pattern: Kidneys and the Heart, and then the Liver and the Lungs.

Begin this practice by smiling into the middle center. See a glowing yellow or golden color in the solar plexus area. Concentrate and focus your yi in the center of the Middle Jiao. Settle your intention in this center until you feel a vibrant force. The middle center is the location in which all the energies of the organs will be collected and transformed. The transformed energy is a neutral Qi. This Qi will be guided back to the organs to energize them and begin the process of rejuvenation.

When you have completed the solar plexus (middle center) part of this nei dan, move your attention to the Kidneys. The color of the Kidneys is blue-green (like the color of the ocean). Some traditions use the color black or blue. Smile into the Kidneys; visualize a vibrant blue-green color materializing there. Spend as much time as you need on this practice until you see and feel the vibrant color and Qi of the Kidneys.

When you have completed the Kidneys part of this nei dan, move your attention to the Heart. The color of the Heart is red. Smile into the Heart; visualize a vibrant red color materializing there. Spend as much time as you need on this practice until you see and feel the vibrant color and Qi of the Heart.

When you have completed the Heart part of this nei dan, move your attention to the Liver. The color of the Liver is green. Smile into the Liver; visualize a vibrant green color materializing there. Spend as much time as you need on this practice until you see and feel the vibrant color and Qi of the Liver.

When you have completed the Liver part of this nei dan, move your attention to the Lungs. The color of the Lungs is white. Smile into the Lungs: visualize a vibrant white color materializing there. Spend as much time as you need on this practice until you see and feel the vibrant color and Qi of the Lungs.

When you have completed this stage of connecting, visualizing and feeling the vibrant energy of the organs, be aware of all the organs vibrating with their colors and Qi. Spend a few minutes being with all the five organ centers.

This stage of the five shen cultivation grows the favorable energies and colors of the organs. This stage builds the life force in the organ centers, creating the strength and integrity to transform the conditioning, imprints and emotional imbalances that may exist. We can look at this process as greeting our psycho-emotional difficulties with a smiling, loving life force. This smiling, loving energy allows for a more effective transformation.

The Five-Phases Senses

Begin this nei dan by becoming aware of your Kidneys. Focus your intention in the Kidneys. When you feel the Qi of the Kidneys, move your attention (yi) to the ears. Focus on the ears; feel the life force in the ears. The ears are connected to the Kidneys. With practice, you will feel the connection between the Kidneys and the ears. Spend a few minutes in this awareness of the Kidneys and the ears. This is fusion of the water correspondences, which includes the Kidneys, the ears and the zhi spirit.

When you have completed the Kidneys part of this nei dan, move your attention to the Heart. Focus your intention in the

Heart. When you feel the Qi of the Heart, move your attention (yi) to the tongue. Focus on the tongue; feel the life force in the tongue. The tongue is connected to the Heart. With practice, you will feel the connection between the Heart and the tongue. Spend a few minutes in this awareness of the Heart and the tongue. This is fusion of the fire correspondences, which includes the Heart, the tongue and the shen spirit.

When you have completed the Heart part of this nei dan, move your attention to the Liver. Focus your intention in the Liver. When you feel the Qi of the Liver, move your attention (yi) to the eyes. Focus on the eyes; feel the life force in the eyes. The eyes are connected to the Liver. With practice, you will feel the connection between the Liver and the eyes. Spend a few minutes in this awareness of the Liver and the eyes. This is fusion of the wood correspondences, which includes the Liver, the eyes and the hun spirit.

When you have completed the Liver part of this nei dan, move your attention to the Lungs. Focus your intention in the Lungs. When you feel the Qi of the Lungs, move your attention (yi) to the nose. Focus on the nose; feel the life force in the nose. The nose is connected to the Lungs. With practice, you will feel the connection between the Lungs and the nose. Spend a few minutes in this awareness of the Lungs and the nose. This is fusion of the metal correspondences, which includes the Lungs, the nose and the po spirit.

When you have completed the Lungs part of this nei dan, move your attention to the Spleen. Focus your intention in the Spleen. When you feel the Qi of the Spleen, move your attention (yi) to the mouth. Focus on the mouth; feel the life force in the mouth. The mouth is connected to the Spleen. With practice, you will feel the connection between the Spleen and the mouth. Spend a few minutes in this awareness of the Spleen and the mouth. This is fusion of the earth correspondences, which includes the Spleen, the mouth and the yi spirit. Notice that the yi is involved in each step of this nei dan. The condition of the yi is integral in our cultivation.

When you have finished this part of the nei dan, become aware of all five organs and their sensory pairings. Feel their Qi. This practice is the foundation for the rest of this nei dan inner meditation.

The Five-Phases Temperatures

Each of the five organs is susceptible to specific temperatures. Temperature imbalances have an unfavorable influence on their own organs and their correspondences.

Begin this nei dan by smiling into the Kidneys. The temperature of the Kidneys is cold. Feel any cold in the Kidneys or cold in the body. Allow the coldness to manifest. Spend as much time as you need until you feel the cold.

When you have completed the Kidneys part of this nei dan, move your attention to the Heart. The Heart temperature is hot. Feel the heat in the Heart or heat in the body. Allow heat to manifest. Spend as much time as you need until you feel the heat.

When you have completed the Kidneys and Heart portion of

this nei dan, simultaneously bring the cold of the Kidneys and the heat of the Heart together. With your intention, move the cold and heat from the organs to the yellow sphere in the center of the Middle Jiao. This yellow sphere is the earth phase, Figure 8.1 The Collection Points. It is the location/space for transforming the temperatures to a balanced, warm temperature. This transformation of temperature is the first in this fusion cultivation. Draw the temperatures, which are Qi, into the Middle Jiao. Draw the heat from the Heart down into the top of the yellow sphere. Draw the cold from the Kidneys up into the bottom of the yellow sphere. Simultaneously, spiral the energies on the outer portion of the yellow sphere and move them to its center. When you get close to the middle of the sphere, mingle the temperatures, creating a warm temperature. Focus your attention on the center, making small circles, collecting this Qi into a small, condensed Qi formation. This Qi formation is called a pearl, crystal or Qi ball. The process of forming this pearl will be repeated throughout this cultivation. The pearl is the refined essence of the organs and the body.

When you have completed the Kidneys and the Heart portion of this nei dan, smile into the Liver. The Liver is warm. Feel any warmth in the Liver and warmth in the body. (It is common to feel heat in the Liver; when it is imbalanced, it can heat up. If you feel heat in the Liver, continue this nei dan in the same way.) Allow the warmth to manifest. Spend as much time as you need until you feel the warmth.

When you have completed the Liver portion of this nei dan, smile into the Lungs. The Lungs are cool. Feel the coolness in the

Lungs and coolness in the body. Allow the coolness to manifest. Spend as much time as you need until you feel the coolness.

When you have completed the Liver and the Lungs portion of this nei dan, simultaneously bring the warmth of the Liver and the coolness of the Lungs together. With your intention, move the warmth and the coolness of the Liver and the Lungs to the yellow sphere in the Middle Jiao. This yellow sphere is the earth phase. It is the space for transforming the temperatures to a warm, balanced temperature. Guide the temperatures, which are Qi, into the yellow sphere in the Middle Jiao. Simultaneously, spiral the energies on the outer portion of the yellow sphere and move them to its center. When you get close to the middle of the sphere, mingle the temperatures, creating a nice warm temperature. Focus your attention on the center, making small circles, collecting this Qi into a small, condensed pearl formation. This Qi formation is also called a pearl, crystal or Qi ball. This process of forming the pearl will be repeated throughout this cultivation.

Finish this part of the nei dan by feeling a mild temperature in the Spleen. Allow a mild temperature to manifest. This can be in the Spleen, as well as throughout the body. After you feel the mild temperature in the Spleen, gently guide it into the yellow sphere in the Middle Jiao. Mix all the temperatures in the yellow sphere. Mix them by spiraling them with your intention. Spiral 18 times one way, and 18 times the other way. You can spiral in patterns of nine. You can spiral clockwise and then counter-clockwise or counter-clockwise and then clockwise; there is no rigid pattern. Spiral the energy (temperatures) into a small pearl shape in the center of the yellow sphere. Smile into the pearl for a few minutes.

The Emotions

In the classic Chinese medicine books the *Su Wen* and the *Ling Shu*, the emotions and the virtues are presented. These classic texts clearly present how the body and emotions are inseparable, and that each influences the other. The five shen nei dan we are now practicing is a profound practice to transform emotions. Chinese and Taoist medicine has a deep understanding of the influences of emotions. In this part of the five shen nei dan, the focus is on emotions.

Part 1: The Kidneys

Begin this nei dan by becoming aware of your Kidneys. Focus your intention in the Kidneys. When you feel the Qi of the Kidneys, allow any fear to manifest. Allow any repressed, suppressed or existing fear to become conscious. Focus on this fear. Emotions are energy, and in this practice we seek to transform this energy to its original nature. When you feel the fear, move it into the blue-green sphere at the lower portion of the lower dan tian. This area is at Ren 1, Hui Yin, the Meeting of Yin. Figure 8.1 shows the collection points area. It is at the perineum. In five-phases theory and Chinese medicine, fire is Yang and water is Yin. They are Shao Yin pairs. It is the fire correspondences that will assist in transforming the fear. The next part of this cultivation occurs in the Heart.

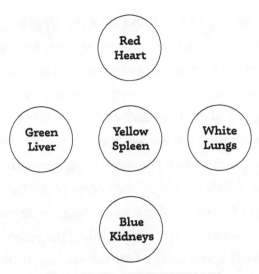

FIGURE 8.1 THE COLLECTION POINTS

Part 2: The Heart

When you have completed the Kidneys part of this nei dan, gently move your attention to the Heart. When you feel the Heart Qi, allow any hastiness, arrogance, impatience and hatred to manifest. When we bury our emotions deep inside our body and mind, they influence deep parts of our being. In Chinese medical terminology, they influence the yuan level. This is the Jing (essence) level and it is our base constitution. To influence the essence level, we need to allow this energy (emotion) to come to the surface, to be transformed to a neutral Qi. When you feel these emotions, move them into the red sphere in the Heart center area (the location is at Ren 17, Tan Zhong).

Part 3: Fusion of the Kidneys and the Heart

When you have completed the Kidneys/zhi and Heart/shen portion of this nei dan, simultaneously bring the emotional energy of the Kidneys and the Heart together. With your intention, move the fear and the hastiness, arrogance, impatience and hatred together into the yellow sphere in the middle center. The process is similar to that used in the temperature part of this nei dan. Guide the emotional energy of the Heart down into the top of the yellow sphere. And then guide the emotional energy of the Kidneys up to the bottom of the yellow sphere. Simultaneously, spiral these emotional energies on the outer portion of the yellow sphere, moving to its center. The movement is from the outer to the inner. As you spiral the emotional energies toward the center, the energies begin to mingle. When you get close to the middle of the sphere, focus on combining these energies together. This yellow or golden sphere of the transforming earth phase allows the emotional energy to transform to its natural, balanced life force. Finish this part of the nei dan by collecting this Qi into a small, condensed pearl formation. Smile to this pearl for a few minutes.

Part 4: The Liver

The next part of this cultivation is to harmonize the Liver/hun and the Lungs/po. Begin this nei dan by bringing your attention to the Liver. When you feel the Liver Qi, allow any anger, irritability and frustration to manifest. Be aware of these emotions. When you feel this emotional energy in the Liver, gently guide it into the green sphere at the Liver collection area. This area is below the Liver at the right side of the body. The area is on the nipple line, at the level of the navel. Draw a line from the navel laterally to a line flowing down from the nipple line. The intersection of these two lines is where the green sphere is located. The area is at the acupuncture point, Spleen 15, Daheng, Great Horizontal. Spiral the emotional energy in the green sphere to collect it there.

Part 5: The Lungs

The next step in this cultivation is to cultivate the Lungs. Begin this nei dan by bringing your attention to the Lungs. When you feel the Lung Qi, allow any sadness, depression, grief and loneliness to manifest. Be aware of these emotions. When you feel this emotional energy of the Lungs, gently guide it into the white sphere at the Lung collection area. This collection area is at the left side of the body, on the nipple line, at the level of the navel. Draw a line from the navel laterally to a line flowing down from the nipple line. The intersection of these two lines is where the white sphere is located. The area is at the acupuncture point, Spleen 15, Daheng, Great Horizontal. Spiral the emotional energy in the white sphere to collect it there.

Part 6: Fusion of the Liver and the Lungs

When you have completed the Liver and Lungs portion of this nei dan, simultaneously bring the emotional energy of the Liver and the Lungs together. With your intention, move the emotional energy of the Liver and Lungs into the yellow sphere in the Middle Jiao. The process is similar to that used with the Kidneys and the Heart. Guide the emotional energy of the Liver and the Lungs into the yellow sphere in the Middle Jiao. Simultaneously, spiral these emotional energies at the outer portion of the yellow sphere, moving to its center. The movement is from the outer to the inner. As you spiral the emotional energies toward the center, their energies begin to mingle. When you get close to the middle of the sphere, focus on combining these energies together. This yellow sphere of the transforming earth phase allows the emotional energy to transform to its natural, balanced life force. The transformed emotional energy of the Kidneys and the Heart is in the yellow sphere; the transformed energy of the Liver and the Lungs is now mixed with these energies. There is a synergy occurring as more of the energies are mixed together. Finish this part of the nei dan by collecting this Qi into a small, condensed pearl formation. Smile to this pearl for a few minutes.

Part 7: The Spleen

Working with the Spleen is the last step of this part of the nei dan practice. Begin this cultivation by becoming aware of your Spleen. Focus your intention in the Spleen. When you feel the Qi of the Spleen, allow any worry, excessive pensiveness and obsessiveness to manifest. Focus on these emotions and imbalances of the Spleen (yi). When you feel these imbalances, move them to the yellow sphere in the middle center. Spiral this energy from the outer aspect of the yellow sphere toward the center. Using your yi, spiral in the yellow sphere. When you continually spiral in the yellow sphere, all the energies of the

Kidneys, Heart, Liver, Lungs and Spleen are fused together into one energy: this is the pearl.

There is a synergy that is created in this nei dan. This process transforms the individual organ and the elemental energy into a refined life force, which rejuvenates the body. This is inner medicine. The next stage of this cultivation is a powerful rejuvenation nei dan. It is a powerful self-healing practice.

Rejuvenating the Organs and the Five Shen

The refined essences of the organs are now in the form of a pearl. This energy is a purified life force and can rejuvenate our body and mind. This final part of the nei dan is to return this refined life force to the internal organs to vitalize and rejuvenate them. This rejuvenation nei dan follows the creation cycle of the five phases. The flow from organ to organ is also called the creation/nourishing five-phases cycle. This nei dan practice guides the energy or life force (the pearl) from organ to organ, until all the organs are nourished. The order is the Kidneys, Liver, Heart, Spleen and Lungs. This pattern is repeated multiple times until you feel the life force in each organ.

Begin this nei dan by smiling and bringing your attention and the pearl into the Kidneys. Allow the pearl to expand to cover the Kidneys. Gently move your attention throughout the Kidneys, filling the Kidneys with a blue-green color. Smile into the Kidneys for a few minutes, until you feel the Kidney Qi. When you decide to continue to the next part of this nei dan, gather the Kidney energy into a pearl and move it to the Liver.

The Liver is a green color. When you move the blue-green pearl of the Kidneys into the Liver, smile into the Liver and allow the blue-green pearl to transform into a green-colored pearl. Allow this green pearl to expand to cover the entire Liver. Smile into the Liver and feel this vibrant Liver Qi. When you decide to continue to the next part of this nei dan, gather the Liver energy into a pearl and move it to the Heart.

The Heart is a red color. When you move the green pearl of the Liver into the Heart, smile into the Heart and allow the green pearl to transform into a red-colored pearl. Allow this red pearl to expand to cover the entire Heart. Smile into the Heart and feel this vibrant Heart Qi. When you decide to continue to the next part of this nei dan, gather the Heart energy into a pearl and move it to the Spleen.

The Spleen is a yellow color. When you move the red pearl of the Heart into the Spleen, smile into the Spleen and allow the red pearl to transform into a yellow-colored pearl. Allow this yellow pearl to expand to cover the entire Spleen. Smile into the Spleen and feel this vibrant Spleen Qi. When you decide to continue to the next part of this nei dan, gather the Spleen energy into a pearl and move it to the Lungs.

The Lungs are a white color. When you move the yellow pearl of the Spleen into the Lungs, smile into the Lungs and allow the yellow pearl to transform into a white-colored pearl. Allow this white pearl to expand to cover the entire Lungs. Smile into the Lungs and feel this vibrant Lung Qi. You can end this nei dan by moving the pearl to the lower dan tian; spiral it there to collect the Qi. If you prefer to continue the nei dan, repeat the cycle three or more times. It is common practice to repeat in multiples of three. Always finish the nei dan by collecting the energy in the lower dan tian.

Suggested Way to Complete this Nei Dan

A powerful way to end this nei dan is to circulate the Qi/pearl in the small heavenly orbit three, six or nine times. This orbit circulation brings a refined and potent life force into the Ren and Du channels and all the channels in the body. It benefits the entire body. If you prefer—and I do suggest that you do so when you can—move the pearl through all the Eight Extraordinary Channels in the pattern presented in this book. After that, collect the Qi in the lower dan tian.

Summary

The *fusion of the five phases* nei dan is a profound inner meditation that clears, transforms and refines our life force. We have three treasures: the physical, mental and spiritual aspects of our life; in Chinese, their names are Jing, Qi and Shen. This five shen cultivation has a profound influence on the imbalances that occur in our life and within each of the three treasures. Imbalances can exist within temperatures, tastes, sensory organs and emotions. This five shen nei dan can transform the effects of the rough and its imprints on our life. It is my favorite nei dan.

Becoming *aware* is a major aspect of the transformation process. This nei dan focuses on creating awareness on each of the correspondences that are in this practice. Becoming aware allows the imbalance to become conscious and provides the opportunity to understand (from an experiencing perspective) and transform the energies. Part of this process is to restore the life force to its normal, natural condition. This is called the yuan (original) condition. Instead of trying to remove the imbalanced energy from the body, we seek to transform the life force. In this way, we do not reduce more of our life force than is necessary, but retain most of it and use it to rejuvenate the body.

The Chinese perceived that each person consists of physical, emotional and spiritual energies. And each person has a level of freedom to decide where to place their attention and their life force. Where we focus our life force is key to how we experience life. We have the free will to focus our attention and create a mindfulness of how we want to live life. The process of focus is the beginning of transformation and nei dan.

The five shen nei dan presented in this book has a profound influence on emotions. In transforming emotions, we become more aware of our life force (energy). When imbalances in our emotional life absorb our life, we have less energy to focus on our spiritual (natural) life. A benefit of this nei dan is that it assists in releasing us from attachments to our emotions and allows us to focus and become aware of our spiritual nature. Spirit is always with us. A goal of nei dan is to clear the rough (stresses, emotions, imprints and conditioning) in our life that requires our life force to maintain it. When this rough is cleared, we can naturally become aware of our spirit.

This awareness will become natural with cultivation. In a way, a new conditioning occurs: our normal and natural way of living is from spirit, not from conditioned responses of the past. The duration required to clear the rough differs with each person. From my experience as a practitioner and teacher, with practice this five shen nei dan (and all the nei dan taught in this book) is a potent way to clear the rough, allowing the natural awareness of spirit within and around us.

CHAPTER 9

Nei Jing Tu—Inner Map

A Guide to the Inner Landscape Map

The Nei Jing Tu is a map of the body and its processes. The map illustrates the transformations that occur during nei dan or certain types of meditation. The ancient insights can be explained in a variety of ways. I present these processes in a practical, clear way that a wide audience can both understand and apply in their personal cultivation (nei dan practice), as well as in clinical practice for healthcare practitioners. Refer to the Nei Jing Tu for a visual of the areas explained.

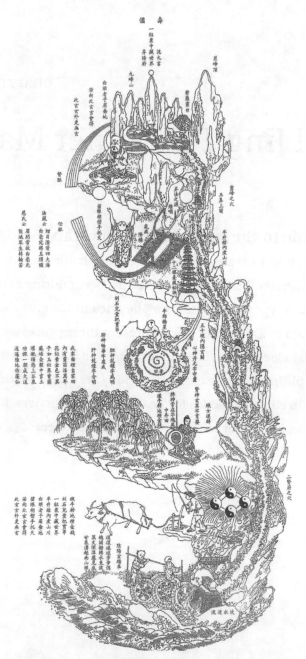

FIGURE 9.1 THE NEI JING TU (INNER LANDSCAPE MAP)

内經圖

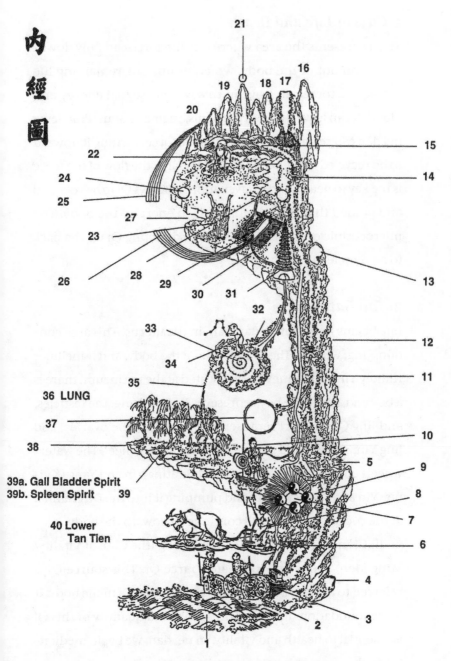

FIGURE 9.2 THE NEI JING TU (INNER LANDSCAPE
MAP) WITH NUMBERED EXPLANATIONS

1. Gate of Life and Death

This represents the area where our life force can flow downward and out of the body, which drains our remaining life force. Life force can leave in this way via sexual energy and blood. It can leave through the penis, vagina or anus. Practicing nei dan can reverse the flow of the life force, turning it upward to be recycled in the body. This reversal of the flow of life force is the key to health and rejuvenation. It allows Qi to be retained and guided through the channels to energize the body. The microcosmic orbit nei dan assists in directing Qi up the back to be recycled in the body.

2. Tail Gate

Life begins in the lower dan tian, in the uterus. This area contains Jing, which is the foundation of the body, and it includes Kidney Yin and Kidney Yang. Located at the perineum, there is a boy and a girl. The boy represents Kidney Yang, the testicles, and Jing Qi. The girl represents Kidney Yin, the ovaries, and Jing Yin. The boy and girl are turning a waterwheel. The waterwheel represents the process of integrating Yin and Yang (Kidney Yin and Kidney Yang) and pumping it into the Du channel at the coccyx, where it will continue to flow up the body.

In Chinese medicine, the body's Yang (the Gate of Vitality/ Ming Men) cooks Jing to create source Qi. This source Qi is referred to as steam. Source Qi is the original Qi in the body. It is the foundation of all Qi. The quality and quantity of this Qi is essential to health and vitality. In nei dan, we begin meditating in this area. This helps to make the steaming process more efficient and effective at producing source Qi. The boy, the girl and the waterwheel represent this process of steaming.

3–4. Sacral Hiatus Gate

The Qi from the Tail Gate flows to the sacral hiatus, Du 2, Yao Shu. This is represented as a rock with eight holes. The rock is the sacrum. The holes in the rock are the eight sacral foramina. The spinal nerves flow into the foramina. An enormous amount of energy flows through this area. These holes are a metaphor for "portals" that receive earth energies, and then blend them with the Kidney Yin and Yang from the Tail Gate. The Sacral Hiatus Gate includes Jing Qi, which includes sexual energy. Jing creates the marrow matrix, which includes marrow and bone. Jing is closely related to bone. Guiding Qi to the sacrum infuses the bone with vitality and enhances Jing. The sacrum represents earth and the lower part of the lower dan tian. Moving vital substances to this area is a type of "marrow washing practice." The sacrum acts as a pump that moves Qi up the spine. This area has a strong influence on Jing, bone, source Qi, fertility and the genitals.

5. Gate of Destiny

The Qi from the Sacral Hiatus Gate moves to the Kidneys and Ming Men, Du 4. The Ming Men is the Gate of Vitality and the fire of the body. This fire (Yang) ignites the process of Yang cooking Yin. The fire cooks Jing, which creates source Qi. This gate has a strong influence on the Kidneys, both Yang and Yin. "Ming" means destiny. In a nei dan context, destiny means the quality of our life force. Nei dan influences the quality of our life. Destiny includes hereditary and ancestral influences. Cultivating this gate and cultivating the entire lower dan tian can release ancestral influences. We can transform and move beyond them. By refining the Qi, the energetics and influences inside Jing are transformed to a neutral state. This is the Qi stage in the Jing–Qi–Shen process.

6. The Cauldron

This is the lower dan tian cauldron. This is where the Ming Men cooks Jing, creating source Qi. This area also activates sexual Qi (which comes from Jing). In nei dan, we bring internal energies together. This cauldron serves to conserve, refine and move them. This cauldron is where we mix and blend our life force to rejuvenate our body. This refined Qi becomes the basis of our life, our awareness, our consciousness.

7. Yin–Yang and Tai Chi

The four Yin–Yang/Tai Chi symbols represent the moving force inside our body. This natural force assists in the transformation of Jing to Qi to Shen. This force activates the Ming Men, the Gate of Vitality. Ming Men cooks Jing, creating steam or source Qi. In nei dan terminology, we call this creation of source Qi "steaming."

NEI JING TU—INNER MAP   167

8. Buffalo Plows the Land and Plants the Golden Elixir

This gate is opposite the navel area, at the back. It is a bridge from the Kidneys, Jing, sexual Qi, source Qi, the Spleen/Stomach center and the yi. It includes the relationship between prenatal and postnatal. When sexual Qi and source Qi move into the Du channel and flow up the spine, source Qi also moves to the earth center/the Spleen and Stomach. Earth is the transforming element. In nei dan, the function of earth is to transform Jing into Qi. This is the first stage in the nei dan process of Jing–Qi–Shen. In Chinese medicine, this center creates gu Qi. Gu Qi then rises up to the Lungs and Heart. This rising of Qi is essential to create Qi and blood in the body. The earth center houses the yi. The yi is our intellectual capacity. It is our thinking and thoughts. The yi filters all experiences of life. It organizes and digests life experiences. Understanding this process enables us to realize how we process life experiences. The nei dan process can assist in changing how we process these experiences. Awareness of the process can also help in releasing ourselves from attachments to old patterns and imprints from early life and from current stresses and intensities. Nei dan refines our life force, the yi, and our filtering process. This refined life force can connect to our yuan shen. This process allows patterns, imprints and stresses to become conscious, allowing them to be transformed. More importantly, we have the opportunity to see them as patterns, imprints and stresses, rather than part of our essential nature. The earth center is the link from the lower dan tian to the upper dan tian.

If stagnations, blockages or other aspects of conditioning are not transformed, they will go to the Heart center. This will subsequently influence our Heart shen.

9. *The True Dan Tian*

This is the location of the Elixir Field. It is the area above the cauldron at the four Tai Chi symbols; it is closer to the spine. This area is where the body's heat creates steam. Qi is represented pictorially as the steam rising from fire cooking rice. This image of steam is an essential aspect of nei dan.

10. *Weaving Maiden Spins at her Loom*

This area is the right Kidney, which is Yin and water. Above the maiden is the cowherder, which represents Yang at the Heart level. The weaving maiden gathers Yin from the body, the stars, the planets and the cosmos. This Yin is then stored in the lower dan tian. One's intention, breath and body (e.g. the eyes) are used to gather and store vital substances in the lower dan tian. This gate is where the Yin of the Kidneys and the Yang of the Heart unite. This unification is the mingling of shen and Jing, which nourishes the transformation of Jing–Qi–Shen.

11. *The Kidney Zhi Spirit*

This area reflects the Kidneys' ability to store prenatal energies, which then transport those energies to support our spiritual development. The Kidneys contain the zhi and willpower. Your willpower helps you live the life you desire.

12. Gate to the One

This area is located opposite the Heart. It is an area where Qi can be drawn into the Heart and the Heart center.

13. The Big Hammer

This is Da Zhui, the Big Hammer, Du 14. It is at the seventh cervical vertebra. It is where all the Yang channels intersect. Da Zhui connects the lower center to the upper center, and then connects the trunk to the arms. This area needs to be clear and free flowing, to let Qi circulate to the upper dan tian and the arms.

14. Cave of the Spirit Peak

This area is Yao Men, Mute's Gate, Du 15. There is an internal pathway that flows from this point to the brain. It has a strong influence on Jing–Shen, the brain. This area guides Qi to the upper dan tian and assists in the transformation of Jing–Qi–Shen. This center assists us in self-expression.

15. Sea of Marrow

The whole head is a mountain with nine caves. The Sea of Marrow surrounds the crown of the head. It includes areas behind, in front of and to the sides of the crown. This area is where heavenly energies flow into our body. An alchemical image includes nine caves. We practice nei dan in these caves and centers.

16. Top of the Great Peak

This area contains the pineal gland, which is an "internal compass" in nei dan. This inner compass connects to the North Star and the center of the sky/celestial. This area connects to heavenly energy. We can make this connection by tucking our chin inward and tilting our head upward.

17. High Place of Many Veils

The High Place of Many Veils is where the spirit and soul can either exit or enter. It is between the Great Peak and the Muddy Pill.

18. Muddy Pill

Muddy Pill is located at Bai Hui, Hundred Meetings, Du 20. When this area is open, it feels like soft mud. It includes the hypothalamus gland. It is a conduit to draw Qi inward, as well as project Qi outward. It connects to the Big Dipper.

19. House of Rising Yang

This is the third eye (Yin Tang). Yin Tang receives energies from the sun and the moon. It is the center of psychic powers, and it is a conduit to the exterior.

20. Nine Sacred Peaks

This location is near the mid-eyebrow. The area includes the pituitary gland; it receives energies to travel in the earthly planes.

21. Immortal Realm

This is the area in front of the crown. The Immortal Realm can draw heavenly energies into the body.

22. Lao Zi

Lao Zi is the Old Man. He is the founder of philosophical Taoism. He is located in the celestial (head), and his long, white beard flows to the earth. Lao Zi is a living embodiment of the unity of heaven and earth. As he lives in the Way (the Tao), he becomes the Way.

23. Heaven and Earth Destiny

This is Damo extending his hands up to connect to the heavenly energy. Damo and Lao Zi are the founders of philosophical Taoism and Chan Buddhism (Chinese Buddhism). Both represent the integration of our heavenly and earthly destination.

24. Sun and Moon Within

The two circles above Damo are the sun and the moon. They are Yang and Yin. The sun and the moon are also the left and right eyes. By moving the eyes in nei dan, we move the Yang and Yin energies in the body. The eye movement integrates and mingles Yang and Yin, which creates harmony. In nei dan, the eyes are used to look inside the body. This "looking" guides Qi. Looking focuses our mind's attention and is the first step in the spinning process. Looking is called the inner eye and inner seeing. The process of spinning creates a movement of Qi, which also commonly causes the body to move in a spinning or circular way. That body movement includes the real eyes too. The mind and body will move together, it's a natural process. Nei dan practitioners will synchronize the eyes and the body spinning movement to enhance the effect of the gathering, circulating and collecting Qi.

25 and 26. Du and Ren Channels

The Du and Ren channels are the major Yin and Yang channels. They are represented here as thick channels lying above, below and in front of Lao Zi. These two channels comprise the microcosmic orbit (small heavenly orbit).

27. The Drawbridge

This is the tongue. It is sometimes called the "Pool of Water." When the tongue touches the palate, it connects the Ren and Du channels. This allows energies to flow through the microcosmic orbit and the three dan tian. This bridge generates fluids, which are the result of nei dan. The fluids change from saliva, to nectar and then to elixir. With practice, the body generates and accumulates increased levels of Qi. This influences the organs, glands and our body fluids. As we cultivate our life force, our Qi and body fluids change.

28. Dew Pond

This area is located behind the soft palate and connects to the pituitary gland.

29. *Mouth Pool*

This is Yin Jiao, Gum Intersection, Du 28. It is the area where the elixir flows from the Dew Pond. Cosmic energy enters here during breathing.

30. *Heavenly Pool*

This is the area where the tongue connects to the palate. This area brings saliva to the palate.

31. *The Pagoda*

This is Tian Tu, Heaven's Chimney, Ren 22. It is located in the space at the top of the sternum. The Qi flowing in the heavenly orbit flows down the throat through this area to nourish the Heart.

32. *Flaming Balls of Fire*

This area is around the "Cowherder Boy Connects to the Stars" (see 34 below). It represents the nei dan cultivation at the Heart center. This nei dan contains the fire and passion of our quest for self-realization.

33. *Spiral of Rice Grains*

The rice grain is a metaphor for the microcosm. All of life is inside each person. Learning to focus our life with nei dan enables us to understand both heaven and earth. The ways of earth are called nature. The ways of heaven are called destiny. The way of the Tao is the cultivation and integration of both heaven and earth, which allows one to enjoy the fruits of all aspects of life.

34. Cowherder Boy Connects to the Stars

This area reflects the connection of the Heart shen, love and compassion. The stars reflect our connection to the Big Dipper and the heavenly realm. Aligning to the Big Dipper during the year enables us to connect to and gather heavenly energies, to support our nei dan practice.

35. Milky Way

This is a bridge connecting the Heart and the Kidneys, connecting the Yang and Yin, and connecting the water and fire. The Heart and the Kidneys are Shao Yin. This connection reflects Jing seeking shen, and it reflects the will for self-realization. The Milky Way merges the Kidney zhi and the Heart shen.

36. Lung Spirit

The Lung spirit represents the value of releasing. When the Lungs inhale, they fill with cosmic Qi; when they exhale, they empty. Emptying is essential to health, vitality and self-realization. Being empty allows each breath, and each moment, to be new and rejuvenating.

37. Solar Plexus

The solar plexus is the middle dan tian. It includes the Spleen, Stomach, Liver, Gallbladder, and the hun and the yi.

38. Outer Ring of the Forest

This area is the edge of the rib cage. It is where the diaphragm is housed.

39. Liver Spirit

The trees are the wood element, and they correspond to the Liver. The Liver stores and transports Qi and blood. Its function includes creating the smooth flow of Qi and blood. It also supports the smooth flow of emotions. The Kidneys are the water element. They nourish wood and the Liver, which in turn nourishes the Heart: this is wood nourishing fire. The Liver is the general, and a good general has a good plan. Nei dan cultivation reveals a plan and a direction in life.

39a. Gallbladder Spirit

This area is in the middle of the Liver. The Liver and the Gallbladder open to the eyes. The outer eyes are eyesight; the inner eyes are spiritual clarity. The Gallbladder is essential in obtaining clarity. Nei dan cultivates our ability to be clear and decisive.

39b. Spleen Spirit

This location is at the Spleen area. It relates to the yi and the transformation process. Nei dan transforms and refines. As the yi becomes refined with nei dan practice, we are able to be a living expression of the Way/the Tao.

40. Lower Dan Tian

This area represents the alchemy of the lower sea of Qi. "The Cauldron," "Yin–Yang and Tai Chi" and "Buffalo Plows the Land and Plants the Golden Elixir" represent the nei dan process.

The processes in the Nei Jing Tu and our body continue throughout our lifetime. The flow of seas, rivers, streams, springs and wells is the exterior image of the interior flows of vital substances: Jing, Qi, blood and body fluids. Proper flows of water are essential to life and a bountiful harvest. Optimal circulation of the vital substances is a key to health and vitality. The Eight Extraordinary Channels nei dan is a powerful way to assist in creating effective circulation of vital substances. This healthy flow clears the rough, allowing you to see and experience the diamond shining inside. This nei dan assists in fulfilling our life quest of spiritual self-realization.

Bibliography

Harper, D. (2007) *Early Chinese Medical Literature: The Mawangdui Medical Manuscripts*. London: Kegan Paul International.

Lu, H. (1985) *A Complete Translation of The Yellow Emperor's Classic of Internal Medicine and the Difficult Classic*. Vancouver: Academy of Oriental Heritage.

Luk, C. and Yu, K.Y. (1999) *Taoist Yoga: Alchemy and Immortality*. San Francisco, CA: Red Wheel/Weiser.

Maciocia, G. (2006) *The Channels of Acupuncture: Clinical Use of the Secondary Channels and the Eight Extraordinary Vessels*. Oxford: Churchill Livingstone.

McCann, H. (2014) *Pricking the Vessels: Blood Letting Therapy in Chinese Medicine*. London: Singing Dragon.

Ni, H.-C. (1979) *The Complete Works of Lao Tzu*. Malibu, CA: The Shrine of the Eternal Breath of Tao.

Ni, M. (1995) *The Yellow Emperor's Classic of Medicine: A New Translation of Neijing Suwen with Commentary*. Boston, MA: Shambhala.

Ni, Y. (1996) *Navigating the Channels of Traditional Chinese Medicine*. San Diego, CA: Complementary Medicine Press.

Twicken, D. (2011) *I Ching Acupuncture – The Balance Method: Clinical Applications of the Ba Gua and I Ching*. London: Singing Dragon.

Twicken, D. (2013) *Eight Extraordinary Channels – Qi Jing Ba Mai: A Handbook for Clinical Practice and Nei Dan Inner Meditation*. London: Singing Dragon.

Twicken, D. (2014) *The Divergent Channels – Jing Bie: A Handbook for Clinical Practice and Five Shen Nei Dan Inner Meditation*. London: Singing Dragon.

Twicken, D. (2015) *The Luo Collaterals: A Handbook for Clinical Practice and Treating Emotions and the Shen and The Six Healing Sounds*. London: Singing Dragon.

Wang, Z. and Wang, J. (2007) *Ling Shu Acupuncture*. Irvine, CA: Ling Shu Press.

Wu, J. (2002) *Ling Shu or The Spiritual Pivot*. Honolulu, HI: University of Hawai'i Press.

Wu, N. and Wu, A. (2002) *Yellow Emperor's Canon of Internal Medicine*. Beijing: China Science Technology Press.

Yang, C. (2004) *A Systematic Classic of Acupuncture and Moxibustion*. Boulder, CO: Blue Poppy Press.

Yang, J.C. (2005) *Shen Disturbance: A Guideline for Psychiatry in Traditional Chinese Medicine*. Self-published.

Index

The Luo Collaterals

A Handbook for Clinical Practice and Treating Emotions and the Shen and The Six Healing Sounds

£31 | $45 | PB | 176PP | ISBN 978 1 84819
230 0 | eISBN 978 0 85701 219 7

First referenced in the Ling Shu and the Su Wen, the Luo Collaterals or Luo Mai, are an integral part of the acupuncture channel system. In this book, Dr David Twicken provides a comprehensive account of the Luo Mai, including detailed analyses of the classical and contemporary theories and clinical applications.

Modern practitioners often use the Luo Collaterals to treat the emotions and the organs, with treatments influencing the blood network, especially the veins and capillaries, along the Luo pathways. Dr Twicken presents a thorough historical analysis of the new theories on which our modern understanding of the Luo Collaterals and Luo points is based and explains the applications. He explores the classical Chinese medical and Taoist interpretation of the Shen, the five Shen and the emotions and provides a comprehensive historical analysis of the Window of the Sky points. Dr Twicken also includes instruction on Healing Sounds Qigong, one of the oldest and most effective forms used to treat the emotions, the internal organs and the five Shen.

An accessible and authoritative guide to the Luo Collaterals, this book will be of immense value to students and practitioners of acupuncture and Chinese medicine, Taiji and Qigong practitioners; and anyone with an interest in Taoist practice.

I Ching Acupuncture –
The Balance Method
Clinical Applications of the
Ba Gua and I Ching

£28.99 | $45 | PB | 272PP | ISBN 978 1
84819 074 0 | eISBN 978 0 85701 064 3

I Ching Acupuncture – The Balance Method is a system of acupuncture point selection based on the principles of Chinese philosophy and classic Chinese texts, including the *I Ching, Nei Jing Su Wen* and *Ling Shu*. In this unique book Dr Twicken presents classic Chinese philosophical models that explain the relationships between philosophy, Chinese medical principles, acupuncture channels and the human body. The models are the He Tu, Luo Shu Nine Palaces, Early Heaven Ba Gua, Later Heaven Ba Gua, Twelve-Stage Growth Cycle, Stems and Branches and the Chinese calendar. These models and theories clearly show the relationships between the acupuncture channels and the human body and provide guiding theory for acupuncture strategies and point selection. I Ching Acupuncture presents six Balance Methods. This clinically effective system of acupuncture is based on minimal and distal acupuncture treatments.

I Ching Acupuncture – The Balance Method is a valuable and effective acupuncture system that can complement any practice.

Eight Extraordinary Channels – Qi Jing Ba Mai
A Handbook for Clinical Practice and Nei Dan Inner Meditation

£26.99 | $45 | PB | 240PP | ISBN 978 1 84819 148 8 | eISBN 978 0 85701 137 4

The Eight Extraordinary channels are amongst the most interesting and clinically important aspects of Chinese medicine and Qigong. This book introduces the theory behind the channels, explains their clinical applications, and explores their psycho-emotional and spiritual qualities. The author also describes how to cultivate the channels through Nei Dan Inner Meditation.

As a practitioner of Chinese medicine or acupuncture, the key to creating effective individual treatment plans is having a wide understanding of channel theory, and a comprehensive knowledge of the pathways and the points on the channels. Dr David Twicken provides treatment strategies, methods and case studies, offering a variety of approaches so as to give the reader a solid foundation from which to confidently create customized treatment plans for each patient.

Offering a historical perspective as well as modern insights, this book will be essential reading for novice as well as experienced practitioners.

The Divergent Channels – Jing Bie
A Handbook for Clinical Practice and Five Shen Nei Dan Inner Meditation

£31 | $45 | PB | 224PP | ISBN 978 1 84819 189 1 | eISBN 978 0 85701 150 3

Rooted in the Su Wen and Ling Shu, Dr Twicken's book integrates Chinese and Taoist medical philosophy, theories, and principles to clearly demonstrate that the Divergent Channels are an essential aspect of the clinical practice of acupuncture. He takes a step-by-step approach to assist practitioners in "working out" the channels, and shows how this versatile channel system can be used in any acupuncture treatment. Twicken also includes instruction on Five Shen Nei Dan inner meditation to help practitioners gain a more profound emotional and spiritual understanding. With case studies and reference to the classic texts throughout, this book provides a complete resource that will help clinicians understand and use the Divergent Channels in clinical practice.

An accessible and comprehensive account of the Divergent Channel system, this book will be a valuable addition to the shelves of students and practitioners of acupuncture and Chinese medicine; taiji and qigong practitioners; and anyone with an interest in Taoist practice.